The Poetics
of Self-Consciousness

The Poetics
of Self-Consciousness

Twentieth-Century
Spanish Poetry

Jonathan Mayhew

Lewisburg
Bucknell University Press
London and Toronto: Associated University Presses

Associated University Presses
440 Forsgate Drive
Cranbury, NJ 08512

Associated University Presses
25 Sicilian Avenue
London WC1A 2QH, England

Associated University Presses
P.O. Box 338, Port Credit
Mississauga, Ontario
Canada L5G 4L8

The paper used in this publication meets the requirements
of the American National Standard for Permanence of Paper
for Printed Library Materials Z39.48-1984.

Library of Congress Cataloging-in-Publication Data

Mayhew, Jonathan, 1960–
    The poetics of self-consciousness : twentieth-century Spanish
poetry / Jonathan Mayhew.
        p.   cm.
    Includes bibliographical references (p.   ) and index.
    ISBN 0-8387-5256-X (alk. paper)
    1. Spanish poetry—20th century—History and criticism.   2. Self
-consciousness in literature.   3. Postmodernism (Literature)—Spain.
4. Poetics.   I. Title.
PQ6073.S45M39   1994
861'.609—dc20   92-56608
                                                                           CIP

PRINTED IN THE UNITED STATES OF AMERICA

Contents

Acknowledgments

The following sections of this book have been appeared as articles in scholarly journals: "Jorge Guillén and the Insufficiency of Poetic Language," *PMLA* 106 (October 1991): 1146–55; reprinted by permission of the Modern Language Association. "'Cuartilla': Pedro Salinas and the Semiotics of Poetry," *Anales de la Literatura Española Contemporánea* 16 (1991): 119–27. "'Límites y espejo': Linguistic Self-Consciousness in the Poetry of Vicente Aleixandre," *MLN* 105 (March 1990): 303–15; reprinted by courtesy of the Johns Hopkins University Press. "The Twilight of the Avant-Garde: Spanish Poetry in the 1980s," *Hispanic Review* (Fall 1992). I am grateful to the editors of these journals for the interest they have shown in my work.

The final writing and revision of the manuscript was completed with the help of a fellowship from the National Endowment for the Humanities. I would also like to thank the College of Humanities, Ohio State University, for a grant that allowed me to do research in Spain during the summer of 1989.

On a more personal note, I am grateful to the many friends and colleagues who have discussed poetry with me over the past few years and offered their material and moral support to this project. Special thanks go to Andrew Debicki, Steve Summerhill, Maureen Ahern and to the department chairs who have supported my research at Ohio State: Don Larson and the late Joe Kubayanda. Joe's untimely death coincided with the completion of my first draft, and I am saddened that I can no longer share his friendship. Without the love, companionship, and intellectual dialogue I have shared with Akiko Tsuchiya, finally, this project might never have come to fruition.

Introduction:
Self-Consciousness in Twentieth-Century Spanish Poetry

One of the most significant aspects of twentieth-century poetry written in the European languages is its linguistic self-consciousness, its awareness of the theoretical problems surrounding poetic language. Students of both French and Anglo-American literature have long recognized the central place of self-consciousness in twentieth-century poetry. Hispanists, in general, have been slower to adopt this perspective, although there have been some significant exceptions in recent years. The aim of this book is to remedy this important gap in the critical literature through a series of theoretically informed readings of representative Spanish poets of the century, from the 1920s through the present.

This study differs in both scope and approach from existing books on twentieth-century Spanish poetry. Debicki's *Poetry of Discovery*, Persin's *Recent Spanish Poetry and the Role of the Reader*, and Soufas's *Conflict of Light and Wind* are treatments of particular groups of writers of the same age, although Soufas argues strongly against the very concept of the literary "generation."[1] No other recent book written in English deals with both prewar and postwar poetry or focuses primarily on poetic self-consciousness. The use of contemporary literary theory is becoming increasingly frequent among students of modern Spanish poetry. Debicki, Persin, and others have used reader-response criticism, structuralism, deconstruction, and similar methods of analysis. I differ from many of these critics, however, in my approach to the poetic text. My primary interest is *poetics*, which I define as the idea of language that is explicitly or implicitly articulated in the poet's work. This interest leads me to de-emphasize poetic language as a purely stylistic phenomenon or even as a means of evoking reader response.

The only full-length study that anticipates this book to a large degree is Silver's *La casa de Anteo*, which also covers a wide range of twentieth-century Spanish poetry, including two of the authors I take up here, and emphasizes poetics.[2] Where I depart from Silver's orientation is in my approach to poetic self-consciousness. He judges Hispanic poets against an a priori model of theoretical awareness, based primarily on Paul de Man's reading of Heidegger. The title of his book refers to the giant of classical myth whose strength derives from his contact with the earth. (Hercules is able to defeat him only by first lifting him into the air.) The implications of this myth for Hispanic poetics are largely negative: with a few exceptions, Silver finds Spanish poets to be telluric and therefore theoretically naive. Poets who do not conform to the Heideggerian model are found wanting. My own approach, in contrast, offers what I hope is a more flexible and generous assessment of the theoretical self-consciousness found in modern Spanish poets. Instead of applying a theory of poetic language to the text, I attempt to view the poets themselves as theoretical thinkers.[3]

The gaps in my study are multiple: I do not attempt an inclusive account of every major development within this period. I exclude, for example, the social, religious, and existential tendencies of the 1940s and 1950s. Since self-consciousness pervades the work of almost every important poet since the turn of the century, my selection of poets is necessarily arbitrary and incomplete: another, equally viable book on the same topic could be written using entirely different poets, or even different works by the poets I do study. My readings are meant to be symptomatic rather than definitive. My intent is to demonstrate a new way of understanding Spanish poetry within the context of the self-consciousness of modern poetry as a whole.

Self-consciousness is characteristic of both the modernism of the first half of the century and the "postmodern" developments of more recent decades. Modernism, in all of its artistic manifestations, is characterized by a close attention to the medium of artistic representation: modern painting explores paint as paint, and modern poetry interrogates the nature of language itself.[4] Since language is inherently semiotic, the modernist purification of the linguistic medium becomes exceedingly complicated. On the one hand, modernist literature is strongly antirealist in orientation: it aims to rid language of its mimetic dimension in order to engage in the free play of the linguistic signifier. Few writers, however, go so far as create such a purified dialect. Since the linguistic sign functions through the relation between signifier and signified, a language stripped of significance would no longer be a language at all.

Instead of purging language of its mimetic and semiotic qualities, then, modernist poets tend to speculate about the relations between signifier and signified and between language and reality. In so doing, they exploit another crucial characteristic of the linguistic medium: its capacity to talk about itself. Words can refer not only to things but also to other words and to language in general. Thus one of the most characteristic forms of modernist poetry is metapoetry, poetry whose subject is itself. Instead of defining modernism as the purification of artistic media, then, it might be more productive to view this purification as a central question to which modernist works address themselves in theoretical terms. The shift from a stylistic to a discursive level of analysis helps to account for the sharp differences of attitude found among modernist poets. The first section of this book consists of three complementary studies of poets who first began to write in the 1920s: Jorge Guillén, Pedro Salinas, and Vicente Aleixandre. Although the three poets manifest a modernist preoccupation with the relation between language and reality, their individual perspectives on the problem of poetic language vary so much that any further generalization would be risky.

Guillén has the reputation of being the prototypically modernist poet within Spanish letters, the writer whose work most clearly and faithfully reflects the "dehumanized" aesthetics of the 1920s. Guillén's poetic thought is atypical of modernism, however, to the extent that it manifests a strong mimetic impulse. The key concept in Guillén's theory of poetic language, developed with great critical acumen in his Charles Eliot Norton lectures at Harvard, is the notion of a perfect adequation between language and reality ("lenguaje suficiente"). Guillén's theory is unable to account for the longstanding tradition of poetic ineffability: poets have long complained that words are inherently incapable of expressing the richness of inner experience. This attitude toward language, which is present in both mysticism and romanticism, becomes especially acute in modern poetry. For Guillén, however, the actual achievement of an adequate poetic language resolves the question: if the poet writes well, his or her distrustful attitude toward language becomes a moot issue.

Although Guillén evades the problem of ineffability in his critical essays, his poetry reflects his awareness that words are not a perfect reflection of the things they purport to represent. Ultimately, Guillén's faith in the representational power of language comes into conflict with his Modernist attempt to create an autonomous artistic medium. Language is not an inadequate representation of reality, as for the poet of the ineffable, but neither is it simply mimetic. Rather, an autonomous poetic language rivals and surpasses the world to which it refers.

Pedro Salinas is a more purely modernist poet than his close friend Jorge Guillén, in the sense that he is more critical of language as a representational medium and more playful in his metasemiotic speculation. Chapter 2 explores Salinas's poetic semiotics with the help of Michael Riffaterre and Umberto Eco. The thesis that Riffaterre expounds in *Semiotics of Poetry*, that literary language is a negation of mimesis, seems made to order for Salinas's early work, in which this negation becomes an explicit theme. I depart from Riffaterre, since I do not consider this antimimetic impulse as an inherent feature of literary language, but as the specific hallmark of poetic modernism, a movement that has its roots precisely in the nineteenth-century French poetry that Riffaterre uses to demonstrate his theory.

In a section of *Semiotics and the Philosophy of Language*, Umberto Eco argues quite cogently that mirror images lack the qualities necessary to be considered signs. In the poetic tradition, however, the mirror has a different status, becoming the most important metaphor both for mimetic representation and for semiotic play. Salinas's metapoetry often takes the form of a self-reflexive look in the mirror of poetic language. The mirror as medium of semiotic self-reflection also appears in the poetry of Vicente Aleixandre, but its meaning becomes quite different: whereas Salinas celebrates the distance between reality and language, Aleixandre laments the loss of vitality that is inherent in linguistic representation. His critical attitude toward his medium is thus antithetical to the aesthetic purism of Salinas's modernist poetry.

The second half of this book considers more recent Spanish poetry under the general rubric of "postmodernism." This term is difficult to define and to apply in a consistent way. Not only is there no critical consensus as to the definition of postmodernism, but it is not at all clear that the most influential theorists of the postmodern are referring to the same phenomenon. The uses of the term in philosophy (Lyotard's critique of "metanarratives"), literary theory (Derrida's deconstruction), and Marxist theory (Jameson's "Cultural logic of late capitalism") are not necessarily homologous with the more exclusively literary applications of the term, such as Perloff's "indeterminacy" and Hutcheon's "historiographic metafiction."[5] Students of postmodern literature do not even agree on a corpus of texts that would qualify as postmodernist: the postmodernists of one critic are often the "late modernists" of another.

In view of this terminological confusion, I have chosen to study several variants of postmodern Spanish poetry without attempting to arrive at a single, unified theory of postmodernity. It seems especially problematic to apply the label to poets who began their literary careers before the advent of "postmodernism" as a concept of literary history. An earlier writer can be a postmodernist without knowing it, of course, but the label seems more appropriate to writers who adopt postmodernism as a self-conscious and clearly recognizable position. The issue here is not merely semantic. The Spanish poets who began to write in the 1950s, for example, fit some definitions of postmodernism, but not others. José Angel Valente, the subject of chapter 4, reflects the urge "to purify the language of the tribe." His idealization of poetic language is logocentric in a quite literal way: he conceives of the Word as the dwelling place of the sacred. The postmodern impulse in Valente's work stems from the absence of a theology behind his logology. Although he glorifies the religious function of poetic language, he cannot put his faith in the referents of this language.

Antonio Gamoneda, a poet who has only recently received critical attention after many years of geographical isolation, shares

Valente's logocentrism. Both poets keep alive the tradition that sees the poet as a prophetic figure and poetic language as a semi-divine calling. For Gamoneda as for Valente, however, poetic language has lost its ultimate foundation in the truth. The poet's voice, while maintaining its powerful rhetoric, simultaneously flaunts its fictive status. Gamoneda's *Descripción de la mentira*, an important long poem, explores the contradictions inherent in poetic language as both a truth-telling and a deceitful discourse.

The lack of a solid foundation for discourse is, of course, an important concern in postmodern literature. Gamoneda's attitude toward language is reminiscent of Richard Rorty's definition of "liberal irony." What should not be forgotten, however, is that linguistic indeterminacy was also a modernist preoccupation. One surprising development in recent criticism is that the commonplaces once applied to modernist literature have now become attributes of postmodernism, while modernism itself has become stereotyped as a monolithic and aesthetically conservative movement. Part of the confusion stems from a too easy equation between modernism and modernity, where modernity is understood in the Habermasian sense as the enlightenment project of rationality. Neither modern nor postmodern poets put their faith in this enlightenment project. The literature that is usually termed "modernist" usually represents a crisis of rationality rather than its apotheosis. Twentieth-century literature, in both its modern and postmodern modalities, reflects the preoccupations of postmodern philosophy, which stems from nineteenth-century figures such as Nietzsche.

Jaime Gil de Biedma, a contemporary of Valente and Gamoneda, renounces all claims to a transcendent poetic discourse. His poetic project thus appears to be somewhat less ambitious than that of many other poets of his generation. His lack of faith in the prophetic function of poetic language makes him a more postmodern poet in some respects. Yet he has affinities with the aesthetically and politically reactionary branch of modern Anglo-American poetry. In an epigraph to *Moralidades*, he cites Yvor Winters's claim that poetic language serves as an instrument of rational control and moral judgment. Gil de Biedma's postmodern skepticism toward language thus bears an odd resemblance to the reactionary antimodernism of the controversial American poet-critic. Although he does not share Winters's reactionary and theocentric opinions, Gil de Biedma views poetic language as a lucid instrument for an ethical self-critique.

The Spanish poets who began to publish in the late sixties or early seventies, who are known as the *novísimos*, are more obviously postmodern in their attitudes than the poets of Gil de Biedma's generation. The chief focus of the *novísimos'* self-consciousness is the literary tradition itself. Their characteristic form of self-consciousness is "culturalism" the obsessive citation of literary and artistic intertexts that has dominated Spanish poetry for the last twenty years. The attitude of these poets toward the Western tradition is deeply ambivalent: they combine an encyclopedic knowledge of literature, art, and music with a sense that high culture is no longer viable in a postmodern age. The principal problem that concerns them is their own relation to the artistic past.

I have chosen two very different poets, Guillermo Carnero and José María Alvarez, in order to illustrate the multiple positions taken by the *novísimos*. Carnero is an intellectual poet who uses cultural artifacts from the past as "ideas of order," models for imposing a rationality onto an irrational reality. Carnero views the imposition of rational order as an arbitrary and irrational act of human will, since reality itself is incommensurate with human knowledge. At the same time, however, this mental activity is inescapable, since there is no other way of understanding reality available. José María Alvarez's deliberately excessive and obsessive culturalist intertextuality takes a different form. His preferred texts are personal talismans rather than models of rationality. A comparison with the contemporary American poet Frank O'Hara illuminates the status of Alvarez's Spanish postmodernism, which reflects a sense of belatedness with respect to the cultural monuments of the past.

As a group, many young Spanish poets of the 1980s share a neotraditionalist aesthetic that departs from the more ambivalent attitude toward tradition among the *novísimos*. If postmodernism implies an avant-garde spirit, then this label should not be applied to the younger Spanish poets. On the other hand, much of their work does answer to the disparaging description of postmodernism put forward by Fredric Jameson. For the Marxist cultural critic, postmodernism is not avant-garde experimentation but neotraditional conservatism, an uncritical and ahistorical recycling of literary and cultural traditions. I prefer to analyze this "neotraditionalism" as *kitsch,* in the special sense that Umberto Eco has given to the term.

The primary intention of this book is not historical; it does not propose to trace the chronological development of self-consciousness in twentieth-century Spanish poetry. There are, however, several general conclusions that arise from my readings of major poets of different periods and generations. In a brief "Afterword," I suggest a new way of understanding the similarities among otherwise dissimilar poets of the same period, such as Salinas, Guillén, and Aleixandre. Instead of deploying the traditional concepts of period style and group aesthetic, I hypothesize that poets beginning their literary careers at the same time often face a common set of theoretical problems. Language, of course, is a concern for all three groups of poets studied in the book, but each defines the problem of language in a different way. For the poets of the 1920s, the central issue is representation: the mimetic relation between language and reality. Valente, Gil de Biedma, and Gamoneda are preoccupied with the ethical and social legitimacy of poetic discourse. The most recent Spanish poets, finally, attempt to rethink their own relation to the cultural and literary tradition itself.

1

Jorge Guillén and the Insufficiency of Poetic Language

Jorge Guillén's *Lenguaje y poesía*, one of the first critical works written in Spanish to address the theoretical problems involved in defining poetic language, has provided a convenient point of departure for subsequent Spanish poets and critics. The most significant innovation in Guillén's lucid exposition of these problems is his linking poetic language to the conception of language that underlies the writing of the poem: "Una obra literaria se define tanto por la actitud del escritor ante el mundo como por su manera de sentir y entender el lenguaje" ["A literary work is defined both by the attitude of its author toward the world and his way of feeling and understanding language"].[1] In his masterful readings of Spanish poetry, Guillén focuses on each poet's implicit vision of language, deftly supplementing traditional stylistic criticism with a subtle examination of relevant metastylistic issues.

Although Howard Young succinctly summarizes the content of *Lenguaje y poesía*, and critics cite it in their readings of Guillén's poetry, no one has thoroughly scrutinized the overall argument of the work.[2] In his perspicacious appreciations of five major Spanish writers, Guillén advances a thesis about the adequacy of language to convey the poet's experience of reality. For Guillén, faith in the power of language is the poetic attitude par excellence. His major task, then, is to explain the stance of two major Spanish poets who seem to deny the primacy of words. Both San Juan de la Cruz and Gustavo Adolfo Bécquer identify the essence of poetry with what they regard as their ineffable preverbal experience, thus introducing a separation between language and experience that Guillén finds intolerable.

To counter the problem of ineffability, Guillén excludes authorial intention from consideration. If the poet ultimately succeeds in using language, then any previous distrust of the medium becomes an extraneous biographical fact. San Juan's masterful style, for example, gives the lie to his belief that mystical experience is inexpressible. By thus disposing of the issue, Guillén allows for only one genuinely poetic attitude toward language: to be a poet is, necessarily, to have faith in the word.

Guillén's exegetes have generally assumed that the theory put forward in *Lenguaje y poesía* corresponds to Guillén's own practice as a poet. A reading of his criticism alongside his poetry, however, reveals two contradictory definitions of "sufficient language." On the one hand, Guillén finds language sufficient as a representational medium: the words of the poem correspond faithfully to the poet's experience. On the other hand, in contrast to this straightforwardly mimetic theory, he wants his own language to be self-sufficient, independent of any represented reality. In several poems from *Cántico*, his most significant work, he views poetic language as an autonomous object that replaces what it purports to represent.

Two complementary binary oppositions structure *Lenguaje y poesía:* "prosaic" versus "poetic" language and "insufficient" versus "sufficient" language. The first opposition concerns poetic diction, the degree of differentiation between the lexicons of poetry and ordinary discourse. The representative of prosaic language, the thirteenth-century poet Gonzalo de Berceo, uses a vocabulary and syntax that are indistinguishable from those of everyday speech. According to Guillén, this plain style is possible because Berceo's medieval worldview does not separate quotidian reality from the divine. Berceo's poetry expresses "la absoluta armonía de la tierra y el cielo, del hombre y Dios, y todo merced al justo lenguaje en que esa armonía se descubre" ["the absolute harmony of earth and heaven, of man and God. And all of this is due to the exact language through which this harmony is revealed"] (15; 5). Immediacy and a complete absence of irony characterize both his worldview and his language: "Ninguna duda, ninguna crítica, ninguna vacilación irónica, ninguna nube de ambigüedad se interponen entre su fe y el mundo" ["No doubt, no criticism, no ironical vacillation, no cloud of ambiguity, interpose themselves between his faith and the world"] (18; 7). Within the larger argument of *Lenguaje y poesía,* Berceo represents a prelapsarian state of linguistic consciousness, in which there is almost no distance between words and things. In Derridean terms, such a view of language is a textbook illustration of the "metaphysics of presence" that characterizes Occidental thought. Although Guillén stresses Berceo's artistry, refuting any notion of primitivism, he implies that Berceo, the first nonanonymous poet in Spanish, embodies the primal unity of language and reality. The term *prose* comes to connote such a unity: "Llamar prosaica la lengua de Berceo adolece de impropiedad anacrónica, a no ser que 'prosaísmo' pierda sus connotaciones negativas, y 'prosa' abarque la unidad esencial de expresión que corresponde a la unidad esencial de concepción" ["To call Berceo's language prosaic is anachronistic, unless 'prosaic' is divested of its negative connotations, and 'prose' is made to embrace the essential unity of expression corresponding to general unity of concept"] (36–37; 22).

Guillén's argument here is similar in intent to William Wordsworth's idea, in the preface to the *Lyrical Ballads,* that poetry does not require a special vocabulary to set it apart from ordinary language. Throughout *Lenguaje y poesía* Guillén expresses a preference for the more particular "lenguaje del poema" rather than the generic "lenguaje poético": "La poesía no requiere ningún especial lenguaje poético. Ninguna palabra está de antemano excluida; cualquier giro puede configurar la frase" ["Poetry does not require any special poetic language. No word is excluded in advance; any expression can give shape to the phrase"] (252; 214). His sympathy for Berceo's prosaic language is obvious. The poetic philosophy that he attributes to the medieval poet—a fusion of the miraculous and the everyday—is reminiscent of the one that critics have applied to the "maravillas concretas" ["concrete marvels"] of Guillén's *Cántico.*[3]

While strongly endorsing Berceo's "prosaic language," Guillén shows equal enthusiasm for Góngora, whose poetic language represents the opposite pole, the most extreme example of a vocabulary deliberately fabricated to be as far removed as possible from ordinary speech. Such evenhandedness is appropriate in a celebration of Spanish poetry that was prepared for an American audience at Harvard University. The seventeenth-century poet's rigorous exercise of his craft and his metaphorical brilliance, anticipating the vanguard images of Guillén's time, merit praise even though Guillén takes issue with the position that Góngora and his contemporaries advocate: "Aquellos humanistas, aquellos poetas no veían, no querían ver cómo la lengua común, *siempre fenómeno estético,* puede elevarse a poesía si esas palabras son proyectadas poéticamente. No es cuestión de vocabulario sino de modo" ["Those humanists and poets did not see—they refused to see—that ordinary language, *always an aesthetic phenomenon,* can be elevated into poetry simply by using its words poetically. The question is not one of vocabulary but of manner"] (49; 32; emphasis added). Despite Góngora's lack of interest in everyday speech, Guillén includes him within the much more general category of poets who demonstrate confidence in language: "Sin una gran fe en las palabras no las habría buscado y elegido con tanto fervor" ["Without his great faith in words he could not have sought and selected them with the fervor he did"] (185; 159). This assertion begs the question of what it means to have faith in words, since Guillén argues that Berceo, who did not fabricate a specifically poetic vocabulary, also exemplifies this faith. Góngora's impassioned search for a poetic language, in other words, could equally well indicate a *lack of faith* in everyday language, a baroque rupture with the medieval faith in the unity of language and experience.

In the remaining chapters of *Lenguaje y poesía* the opposition between the prosaic and the poetic gives way to a second contrast between two views of the efficacy of the poetic word. Guillén's first opposition concerns the question of whether poetry requires a language of its own; his second operates at a higher level of abstraction, further removed from the formal features of the text. The distinction is not between two types of discourse but between two attitudes toward language. Guillén asks whether language is capable of expressing the richness of the poet's inner experience. He portrays all of the writers studied, including those who believe language to be insufficient, as superior stylists. What divides the poets of the ineffable from the believers in the adequacy of the word is not any formal feature but the distinctive way in which the two groups formulate the relation between language and experience.

Two poets, the mystic San Juan de la Cruz and the romantic Gustavo Adolfo Bécquer, represent the group that views experience as essentially ineffable, untranslatable into any linguistic medium. Although Guillén admires both writers, he diverges from their vision of language. In his attempt to explain their efficacious use of language, he suggests that their poetic expression is adequate despite their skepticism toward language. San Juan de la Cruz's poems are inadequate only when they are read according to the author's stated intentions, as expressions of a mystical experience that is by definition ineffable. Guillén remains unconvinced by the allegorical commentaries that San Juan wrote in order to explain the religious significance of his poetry. As expressions of secular love, in contrast, these poems succeed admirably:

> Concluyamos, pues, que San Juan de la Cruz, el mayor poeta entre todos los místicos, compuso poemas que se suelen considerar místicos atendiendo a la biografía y a la alegoría, segun una lectura poético-prosaica, que superpone a los versos los comentarios. La lectura poética en esta ocasión—ejemplar—no tiene nada que abstraer de los poemas, que lo son, y admirables, sin contener biografía ni alegoría. (136)

> This brings us, then, to the conclusion that San Juan de la Cruz, the greatest poet of all the mystics, composed poems which it is customary to call mystical for reasons that are biographical and allegorical, on the basis of a combined reading of the prose and poetry which superimposes the commentaries on the verses. Our purely poetic reading does not take anything away from the poems, which are indeed poems, and admirable ones, without biography or allegory. (114)

Guillén draws a similar distinction between Bécquer's superb poetic results and his explicit poetics. Bécquer identifies "poetry" with a state of mind that precedes the actual writing. Glossing Bécquer's lines "Podrá no haber poetas; pero siempre / habrá poesía" ["There might be no poets; but there will always be poetry"] Guillén responds: "Sólo habrá poesía cuando el espíritu sea forma, plenitud de palabras. De lo inefable, por supuesto, no puede hablar sino el autor. Al lector no le concierne más que el texto, incompatible con cualquier escrutinio comparativo entre la prepoesía de la Creación y esta segunda creación que es el poema" ["There will be poetry only when the spirit becomes form, the plenitude of the word. Of the ineffable, of course, only the author can speak. The reader is concerned only with the text, which is incompatible with any comparative study of the prepoetry of the Creation and this second creation that is the poem"] (173; 147–48). This rigorous distinction between the author's experience or intention and the reader's subsequent confrontation with the text is sensible enough: the reader has access only to the results of Bécquer's art, not to the rich subjectivity of the poet's experience. Guillén's New Critical exclusion of intentionality, however, blinds him to the potentially productive force of an author's poetics. The theory of language implicit in the work becomes, in Guillén's account, a poetically inert biographical circumstance. Guillén presents the success of Bécquer's poetry as a virtual disproof of Bécquer's poetic theory: "Pese a tantas dificultades, el poeta, quizá descontento, acaba por entregarnos, sumo dicente, la victoriosa expresión" ["But in spite of all these difficulties, the poet—dissatisfied, perhaps, but still the supreme sayer—delivers to us at last his victorious expression"] (177; 151).

Guillén chooses a prose writer, the twentieth-century lyrical novelist Gabriel Miró, to illustrate the opposite pole from the two poets of the ineffable. The reservations that the reader senses in his treatment of San Juan and Bécquer give way to an unmitigated celebration of Miró's work. In Miró, as in Berceo, he finds a harmony between language and experience. He does not, however, reduce Miró's poetics to a simple theory of adequate representation; language does not replicate reality but supplements and completes it. Whereas language is a subtraction from experience for San Juan and Bécquer, for Miró it is an addition, without which the "original" experience would be inadequate: "No es sólo que la contemplación pueda encontrar su expresión adecuada. Miró dice más: el acto creador se realiza del todo gracias al acto verbal" ["It is not simply that contemplation may find adequate expression for itself. Miró says more than this: the contemplative act is wholly realized thanks to the verbal act"] (186; 160).

Both of Guillén's oppositions—between "prosaic" and "poetic" language and between "insufficient" and "sufficient" language—concern the distance between language and reality. It is curious, then, that Guillén juxtaposes the oppositions without explicitly comparing them. Had he examined their intersection, he might have seen that "insufficient language" is open to several interpretations. One might hold that language is irreversibly inadequate, notwithstanding the poet's efforts. This is the position that Guillén attributes to San Juan and to Bécquer. A contrary view is that the poet's craft compensates for the insufficiency of ordinary language. Gérard Genette has called this idea "secondary Cratylism."[4] While a Cratylist, named after the character in Plato's *Cratylus*, believes in the natural motivation of the sign, the mimetic relation between the signifier and the signified (best exemplified by onomatopeia, or sound symbolism), a secondary Cratylist recognizes that the linguistic sign is arbitrary but attempts to remedy this arbitrariness through poetic language. Genette ascribes this position to Mallarmé: "The nonmimetic character of language is thus, in a certain way, the opportunity and the condition for poetry to exist. Poetry only exists to 'remunerate,' in other words, to repair and compensate for the 'defect of languages.'"[5]

In *Lenguaje y poesía* Guillén vacillates between two alternatives: (1) Berceo's view that language in a relatively raw state is adequate for poetry; (2) Góngora's belief that in its ordinary, prosaic manifestations, language is insufficient for the expression of experience, but that the poet can elaborate a specifically poetic language for that purpose. While Guillén would probably consider Berceo's poetics unworkable in a more ironic age, he also opposes the baroque attempt to construct a special lexicon for poetry. He identifies most closely with the poetics of Gabriel Miró, the only twentieth-century writer in his study. It is interesting that Guillén twice links the idea of linguistic sufficiency to prose, first to the prosaic verse of Berceo and subsequently to the poetic prose of Miró. The writer who has faith in the word presumably does not need to compensate for its insufficiency by creating a poetic language wholly distinct from everyday speech. For Guillén, poetic and prosaic language do not stand in an absolute opposition. The difference between them is one of degree: the language of the poem is simply a more carefully selected and refined version of the already adequate language of everyday life.

Guillén takes San Juan's and Bécquer's apparent lack of faith in language at face value, as an absolute denial of the efficacy of words, and considers no other interpretation. Conceivably, however, an author's concern with linguistic insufficiency could act as a positive factor within poetic discourse. That is, the poetics of insufficient language might be a form of secondary Cratylism, the idea that poetry compensates for the intrinsic inadequacy of language. Bécquer's protest that words cannot contain the richness of experience could be understood in this way. In the very act of making this protest, Bécquer might be subtly summoning forth a second, ideal, language, one containing "palabras que fuesen a un tiempo / suspiros y risas, colores y notas" [words that would be at once / sighs and laughs, colors and notes"].[6] Although the romantic poet depicts this language as a desire that cannot be fulfilled, he simultaneously evokes its possibility in the reader's imagination.

In its most radical version, secondary Cratylism makes the defectiveness of language the very source of poetry's efficacy. Thus the negative pole of insufficiency becomes identified with a more profound linguistic power. This identification occurs in the poetics of a major poet of a younger generation, José Angel Valente, who has rethought Guillén's distinction thoroughly. In an important essay entitled "La hermenéutica y la cortedad del decir" ["Hermeneutics and the shortness of speech"], Valente examines the centrality of the ineffability topos in modern poetics. Not coincidentally, he examines this theoretical problem in the poetry of San Juan de la Cruz:

La experiencia de lo que no tiene forma busca el decir, se aloja de algún modo en un lenguaje cuya eficacia acaso esté en la tensión máxima a que lo obliga su propia cortedad. En el punto de máxima tensión con el lenguaje, con el lenguaje en vecindad del estallido, se produce la gran poesía, donde lo indecible como tal queda infinitamente dicho.[7]

The experience of what does not have form searches for speech, inhabits in some way a language whose efficacy perhaps resides in the maximum tension to which its own inadequacy obliges it. At the point of maximum tension with language, with language at the point of explosion, great poetry is produced, where the unsayable as such remains infinitely said.

Unlike Guillén, who views the realm of the unsayable as extrapoetic by definition, Valente identifies it as the source of poetic power. Whereas Guillén sees San Juan's poetics of ineffability as a potential obstacle for both poet and reader, Valente attributes the efficacy of poetic language to the tension between language and silence in the mystic's poetic theory.[8]

Given Valente's belief in the paradoxical power of insufficient language, it is not surprising that the younger poet questions Guillén's reliance on linguistic adequacy. For Valente, Guillén's work succeeds because it disconfirms Guillén's poetics. After pointing to the geometrical coherence of Guillén's work, which reflects the harmony of poet, language, and world, Valente flatly denies the poetic value of the older poet's aesthetic credo: "¿No habría que buscar, acaso por vía única, el residuo poético de *Cántico* en sus 'claroscuros,' en las brechas que otro tiempo o poder más real abre, a pesar de todo, en su ajustada geometría?" ["Would we not be obliged to seek (perhaps exclusively) the poetic residue of *Cántico* in its 'chiaroscuros,' in the gaps that another, more authentic time and power opens up, in spite of everything, in its well-adjusted geometry?"].[9]

Despite Guillén's deservedly high reputation as a twentieth-century poet, his unwillingness to recognize the power of ineffability sets him apart from the major current in modern poetry that emphasizes the limits of language. In a move that recalls Guillén's dismissal of San Juan's authorial intentions, Valente suggests that the contemporary reader must salvage Guillén's work by reading it against the grain. Valente's comment reveals a desire to save the older poet from the apparent conservatism of his aesthetics. Guillén is such a prestigious and valuable presence in modern Spanish poetry that subsequent poets cannot simply ignore his work; thus they attempt a rescue operation to salvage his precarious modernity.

Valente does not explicitly identify Guillén's *claroscuros*. Other critics as well as Guillén himself have pointed to the occasional nocturnal poem, or to the growing awareness of historical reality in his later work. In a less literal fashion, I would locate the problem at the heart of Guillén's theory of linguistic sufficiency. The blind spot in this theory is the contradiction between the sufficiency and the autonomy of language. Sufficiency implies the representation of a reality that antedates language. Autonomy, in contrast, would be defined as the ability of language to stand independently from this prelinguistic reality. Guillén argues that the reader has no access to San Juan's inner world and thus no comparative basis by which to judge the success of his poetic achievement. A similar distinction can be applied to Guillén's poetic texts. Most of his critics have assumed that he carries out his stated intentions, that his work is a perfect realization of his poetics of linguistic faith. Guillén's idea that poetic language is independent of its creator's subjectivity, however, implies that the words of a poem form an opaque linguistic screen and that the poet's experience is inaccessible to the reader.

The contradiction between the mimetic and autonomous dimensions of literary language is evident in Guillén's treatment of Gabriel Miró in the culminating chapter of *Lenguaje y poesía*. Citing Plato's *Cratylus*, Guillén portrays Miró as a believer in the natural efficacy of the word (191). Yet the gist of his argument is not that Miró's language is sufficient, but rather that it is self-sufficient, unfettered by the reality that it purports to represent. Language supplements rather than imitates reality, and this supplement in turn implies a gap in the original experience. Guillén cites Miró's words verbatim: "Hay emociones que no lo son hasta que no reciben la fuerza lírica de la palabra, la palabra plena y exacta" ["There are emotions that are not wholly felt until they receive the lyric force of the word, their own full and exact word"] (186; 160).

Mimesis is clearly privileged in the work of critics who employ a phenomenological approach to explain Guillén's "being-in-the-world," at attitude that reflects the influence of Ortega y Gasset's philosophy, though not his idea of the "dehumanization" of modern art.[10] The potential weakness of this approach is its failure to take into account the mediation of language. Critics usually assume that Guillén's style is a straightforward vehicle for the expression of his vision of reality.[11] They do not entertain the idea that the linguistic incarnation of a vital attitude might transform this attitude into something quite different.

Several poems in *Cántico* explicitly reveal this transmutation of vision into language. Two poems in particular, "Los nombres" and "Hacia el nombre," link this process to naming, one of the poet's archetypal tasks:

LOS NOMBRES

Albor. El horizonte
Entreabre sus pestañas
Y empieza a ver. ¿Qué? Nombres.
Están sobre la pátina

De las cosas. La rosa
Se llama todavía
Hoy rosa, y la memoria
De su tránsito, prisa,

Prisa de vivir más.
¡A largo amor nos alce
Esa pujanza agraz
Del Instante, tan ágil

Que en llegando a su meta
Corre a imponer Después!
¡Alerta, alerta, alerta,
Yo seré, yo seré!

¿Y las rosas? Pestañas
Cerradas: horizonte
Final. ¿Acaso nada?
Pero quedan los nombres.[12]

Dawn-whiteness. The horizon
Half opens its eyelids
And begins to see. What? Names.
They are on the patina

Of things. The rose
Is stilled named
Rose today, and the memory
Of its transit, haste,

Haste to live more.
To a long love it lifts us,
This bitter drive
Of the instant, so agile

That in reaching its goal
It runs to impose After!
Alert, alert, alert,
I will be, I will be!

And the roses? Eyelids
Closed: final
Horizon. Nothing perhaps?
But the names remain.

In a revealing reading of this poem, Havard distinguishes Guillén's attitude toward language from that of his symbolist predecessor: "The vital difference from Valéry's treatment is that the poet here does not intercede between language and reality. Rather, the latter literally converge—'Nombres / Están sobre la pátina / De las cosas'—and the poet, with his dawn-eye, simply witnesses this natural union."[13] The union of language and reality, however, is far from total. Words do not become things, but rather adhere to their surface. Furthermore, this convergence is provisional: the speaker is not even certain that the word *rosa* will retain its meaning from one day to the next. Finally, with the dissipation of the poet's vision, which coincides with the fall of night and the closing of his eyes, only words remain. One critic has noted that when the poem was first published in Ortega y Gasset's *Revista de Occidente* the last line read "Sólo quedan los nombres" ["only names remain"].[14] The poet-speaker's original vision of the landscape, insofar as we can speak of it at all, serves as a pretext for the creation of a verbal object that ultimately exists autonomously, after the original experience is reduced to nothing.[15]

"Los nombres" deals directly with the relation between poetic vision and poetic language. Such poems are more frequent in Guillén's *opus* than one would be led to expect. Critics have argued, or simply assumed, that his poetry effaces the mediation of language. Even Silver, who recognizes this mediation in Salinas's poetry, denies Guillén's linguistic self-consciousness: "En Guillén, como sabemos, la represión del tercer término, escritura, es decir, la negativa a reconocer temáticamente la necesaria mediación del lenguaje, es total. La poesía se equipara con el respirar; la poesía es poseer, raptar la realidad" ["In Guillén, as we know, the repression of the third term, writing, in other words the refusal to recognize the necessary mediation of language thematically, is total. Poetry is equated with breathing; poetry is a possessing, a grabbing hold of reality."][16]

In "Hacia el nombre" ["Toward the name"], the poet-speaker's vision of a flower is not complete until its name emerges. As in Guillén's reading of Miró, experience is incomplete without its linguistic supplement:

> Se junta el follaje en ramo,
> Y sólo sobre su cima
> Dominio visible ejerce
> La penetración de brisa.
> Desplegándose va el fuste
> Primaveral. Ya principia
> La flor a colorearse
> Despacio. ¿Sólo rojiza?
> No, no. La flor se impacienta,
> Quiere henchir su nombre: lila.
>
> (*Cántico*, 292)

> Foliage converges in a limb
> And over its heights
> Only the breeze's penetration
> Holds visible dominion.
> Spring wood comes
> Unfurling. Already the flower
> Begins to redden
> Slowly. Reddish only?
> No, no. The flower grows impatient,
> It wants to fill up its name: lilac.

The title of the poem reveals a concern for the process of poetic naming: as the initially anonymous flower blooms, revealing itself as a lilac, the poem itself builds to the climax of the act of naming. These two analogous processes converge in the final word of the poem. Guillén exploits the conventional comparison between plants and poems—implicit in notions like "organic form"—in order to draw a parallel between artistic creation and the blooming that his poem describes. The impatience of the lilac reflects that of the reader, who is anxious to reach the name promised by the title. Guillén's tight-knit form creates the expectation of both semantic and prosodical closure: the much-awaited name also satisfies the poem's assonantal rhyme scheme.

The flower's principal attribute, its reddish color, is insufficient in itself. As the verb *henchir* implies, the actual flower attempts to match up to the expectation created by the space of its linguistic representation. The implied metaphor of language as the container of meaning is traditional. Poets and philosophers of language have often discussed the adequacy of words, the appropriateness of particular sounds for representing objects in the world, and Genette's *Mimologiques* exhaustively chronicles such efforts. In "Hacia el nombre," however, Guillén inverts the usual concern with the motivation of the linguistic sign: here it is the natural object that aspires to be an adequate bearer of the name *lila*. Guillén's poetic credo is often assumed to be naively mimetic: words suffice to represent reality. In this ingenious inversion of Cratylism, however, the author of *Cántico* reveals that he is more concerned with the adequacy of reality to fulfill the promise of language itself.

Texts such as "Los nombres" and "Hacia el nombre" reflect Guillén's persistent obsession with the process of transforming vision into language. This concern is also present, though less obviously, in poems that do not directly allude to the act of naming. In "A lápiz," for example, the poet's instrument reduces referential reality to an abstract visual representation:

> ¿El mundo será tan fino?
> ¿Lo veo por nuevas lentes?
> Hay rayas. Inteligentes,
> circunscriben un destino,
> Sereno así. Yo adivino
> Por los ojos, por la mano
> Lo que se revuelve arcano
> Bajo calidad tan lisa.
> Toda un alma se precisa,
> Vale. Tras ella me afano.

(*Cántico*, 236)

> Could the world be so fine?
> Do I see it through new lenses?
> There are lines. Intelligent,
> They circumscribe a destiny,
> Calm like this. I guess
> Through my eyes, through my hand

> What is agitated, arcane
> Under so smooth a quality.
> An entire soul becomes precise,
> Worthy. In its pursuit I strive.

The rather abstract language of the poem allows for a productive ambiguity: the pencil can be used for either drawing or writing, artistic or literary representation. (The word *rayas* normally refers to the lines of ruled paper.) In either pursuit, the artist-poet's eyes and hand improve upon the world, depicting it in finer lines. Since the objects represented remain vaguely defined—"el mundo," "toda un alma"—the reader's attention is focused instead on the process of representation. The poet's desire to define reality as precisely as possible gives way to a self-conscious preoccupation with the form of this definition. The reader, of course, has no independent access to the poet's experience; he or she perceives a reality that is already mediated through the poet's artistic efforts.

A recognition of Guillén's "hypermimeticism"—his desire to create a language that surpasses rather than merely equals the reality that it depicts—helps to explain a persistent problem in Guillén criticism. Guillén has enjoyed a secure reputation since the publication of the first edition of *Cántico* in 1928. His prestige, however, rests on two potentially contradictory qualities of his work: its formal fabrication, and its vital faith in reality. The exaltation of Guillén's stylistic brilliance, found in numerous formalist and linguistic studies of his work, stands in an uneasy relation to the frequent celebrations of his work as a nonproblematic representation of ordinary reality. I would like to suggest that Guillén's formalism is antimimetic. The great artistic and structural achievement of Guillén's verse does not necessarily make it a more adequate vehicle for the expression of the poet's philosophy. In fact, his preoccupation with the process of naming and representing reality often stands in the way of the uncomplicated faith in representational language that critics have attributed to him. Guillén often views poetic form as an escape from the threatening chaos of reality. As he says in "Hacia el poema," "La forma se me vuelve salvavidas" ["Form becomes my life jacket"] (*Cántico*, 263). His well-studied geometrical metaphors, evident in such poems as "Perfección del círculo" ["Perfection of the circle"] (*Cántico,* 80), tend to convert language into an artifact rather than a mimetic instrument.

Critics have often attempted to dispel the widespread notion that Guillén is an excessively abstract, cerebral poet. Curiously enough, this accusation surfaces only as a fallacy to be refuted: no one still argues in favor of this proposition. In *Lenguaje y poesía,* Guillén himself attempts to put to rest two related clichés pertaining both to his work and to the poetry of the 1920s: "pure poetry" and Ortega's "dehumanization of art" (244–45). The specialists are correct when they deny that Guillén is an "intellectual poet": he does not often wrestle with conceptually complex ideas.[17] The charge of coldness, however, continues to haunt discussions of his work, if only in negative form. This accusation, I would argue, stems from Guillén's foregrounding of language. His champions point to his vitalism, but they do not question the view that language is a transparent vehicle. A contrary reading would consider the highly structured autonomy of Guillén's language as a potential obstacle to the communication of the poet's vision. The great care with which Guillén elaborates his poetic language as an artifact does not ensure that this language will lead the reader into his poetic world.

Guillén himself is aware of this problem in Miró's style, although he attempts to explain it away: "El estilo denso, compacto, jugoso viene a ser la pantalla admirable que todo lo refleja, aunque para algunos lectores constituya un estorbo que no deja trasparentar el contenido" ["His style, terse, compact, pithy, becomes an admirable screen reflecting everything, although for some readers it may constitute an obstruction that does not let the content show through"] (228; 194). Rather than viewing this simultaneous transparence and opacity as a feature inherent in literary language, Guillén privileges mimesis over a potentially opaque autonomy. He condemns those readers who would view Miró's rich language as an impediment to communication: "Hasta para algunos supuestos cultos la página bien escrita resulta página decorativa, y toda forma suena a formalismo" ["Even for some supposedly cultured readers, a well-written page is merely a decorative page, and all form to them smacks of formalism"] (228; 194). Taking a similar position, Havard poses a rhetorical question: "Are we to find . . . an opposition between the real content of Guillén's poems on the one hand, with their jubilantly physical celebration of human life, and, on the other, their severe compositional mode which to some might seem not only unreal, but, exaggerating the analogy, glacial?"[18] Havard attributes this negative view of Guillén's art to two older poets—Antonio Machado and Juan Ramón Jiménez—and goes on to argue against any separation between form and content.[19]

It would be absurd to deny that Guillén's poetic form bears some relation to the content of his vision. I could contend, however, that this relation is a complicated one and that it is impossible to conceive of the poet's "jubilantly physical celebration of human life" as a prelinguistic essence that is subsequently translated into the abstract language of *Cántico*. As Guillén's own logic would dictate, the notion of an organic union between experience and expression begs the question by assuming that thought precedes its linguistic expression. As I have argued in this chapter, Guillén rejects the poetics of ineffability on the grounds that the poet's language must be independent of his or her prepoetic experience. In so doing, he fails to recognize the generative power of linguistic insufficiency. His own belief in "sufficient" language, however, leads him far beyond the mimetic poetics that many critics have celebrated. In the poems of *Cántico* he constructs an autonomous linguistic world that casts a shadow over his apparently unquestioning faith in the power of language to represent reality.

2

Pedro Salinas and the Semiotics of Poetry

"l'homme pursuit noir sur blanc."
"Man pursues black on white."
—Mallarmé

1. "Cuartilla" ("Blank Page")

The highly self-reflexive poetry of Pedro Salinas offers fertile ground for a metacritical examination of poetic semiosis. Students of Hispanic poetry, however, have been slow to adopt theoretical models that might illuminate this aspect of his work. Those critics who have studied Spanish metapoetry have tended to neglect Salinas and other prewar poets in favor of more recent writers, especially those of the 1960s and 1970s. In the pages that follow, Salinas's work will serve as a test case of the semiotics of poetry developed by Michael Riffaterre.[1] The aim is not simply to apply Riffaterrian semiotics to Salinas's texts: such "applications" of pre-established critical methodologies place the critic in a parasitical relation to the theorist. Instead, Salinas will provide the occasion for a reevaluation of Riffaterre's seminal work. A dialectical inter-action between theory and interpretive practice enriches both ac-tivities. The need for this interaction is especially acute in the study of poetry; in contrast to the proliferation of theories ori-ented toward the study of narrative fiction, the semiotics of poetry remains in a relatively inchoate state.

Michael Riffaterre's theory offers a striking reversal of one of the principal tenets of traditional poetics. Poetic language has often been valued as a series of techniques for concentrating or distilling meaning in the fewest possible words. In this scheme of values, redundancy is an aesthetic defect. For Riffaterre, in contrast, the overdetermination of poetic language is its most prominent feature, and poetic "significance" is virtually identical to the absence of meaning: poetry is defined as a language that says nothing—the same nothing—over and over again. In the first chapter of *Semiotics of Poetry*, "The Poem's Significance," Riffaterre adduces a series of "monochromatic" texts. One of these is "Combat de Sénégalais la nuit dans un tunnel" [Night combat of Senegalese tribeseman inside a tunnel], another is "Perdu dans une exposition de blanc encadrée de momies" [Lost at a white sale surrounded by Egyptian mummies].[2] These short texts are exemplary because of their overdetermination. Their various elements do not refer to objects in the world, but rather to a particular linguistic matrix, "blackness" and "whiteness" respectively. Riffaterre defines poetic discourse, then, as "the equivalence established between a word and a text, or a text and another text."[3] The poetic text is essentially monosemiotic, in that its apparently diverse elements all come to refer to a central nucleus of meaning.

Riffaterre's theory of poetic significance is also a theory of interpretation.[4] The reader of the poem progresses from a "mimetic" reading, in which the text is perceived as an imitation of external reality, to a "semiotic" reading, in which he or she identifies the central matrix of the text. This process takes place because of the presence of certain troubling inconsistencies—which Riffaterre calls "ungrammaticalities"—at the mimetic level. Textual details that cannot be explained in terms of their correspondence to reality can only be resolved through poetic semiosis. In the examples above, the reader might wonder why mummies are present at the white sale, or what the Senagalese tribesman are doing in a tunnel. Such apparent incongruities, however, are easily resolved through the identification of the matrix.

Although Riffaterre's theory has generated convincing readings of otherwise difficult texts, it neglects the metasemiotic dimension of the text, that is, the poem's consciousness of itself as a semiotic system. Riffaterre's model maintains the traditional separation between critical "metalanguage" and the "language-object" of the poetic text. The critic's language explains that of the poet, and these two levels of discourse are never confused. As Barthes has pointed out, however, one of the major developments in modern

literature is precisely the blurring of the boundary between literature and literary criticism: "la littérature s'est mise à se sentir
double: à la fois objet et regard sur cet objet, parole et parole de
cette parole, littérature objet et méta-littérature" [Literature has
come to be felt as double: at once an object and a gaze upon this
object, a word and a word of this word, literature-object and
metaliterature"].[5] Not coincidentally, Riffaterre's poetic examples
are primarily nineteenth- and twentieth-century French poems,
texts from the period in which Barthes situates this ascent of
metaliterature. Mallarmé, the figure to whom Barthes attributes
"la volonté héroïque de confondre dans une même substance
écrite la littérature et la pensée de la littérature" ["the heroic will
to combine in an identical written substance literature and the
theory of literature"] is an important figure in *Semiotics of Poetry*,
as are other French symbolist poets.[6] Riffaterre's neglect of the
metasemiotic dimension of the poetic text is especially striking
given that many of his own examples reveal an explicit concern
with the nature of poetic language. A re-vision of his work might
shift the emphasis from the *semiotics* of poetry—a metalanguage
applied to the poetic object—to the semiotics of *poetry:* poetic
language as a reflection on itself. Modern poets are semioticians
in their own right, not simply because they transform experience
into signs, but because they do so in a language that necessarily
reflects upon this very process.

Pedro Salinas is an erudite Spanish postsymbolist poet, an heir
to Mallarmé's self-conscious art. Thus it is not surprising that his
poetry exemplifies the fusion of poetic semiosis and metasem-
iosis. The initial poem of *Seguro azar* [Certain chance] (1931), Salinas's second book of poetry, illustrates the monochromaticism
that Riffaterre uses to demonstrate the overdetermination of literary language:

CUARTILLA

Invierno, mundo en blanco.
Mármoles, nieves, plumas,
blancos llueven, erigen
blancura, a blanco juegan.
Ligerísimas,

escurridizas, altas,
las columnas sostienen
techos de nubes blancas.
Bandas
de palomas dudosas
entre blancos, arriba
y abajo, vacilantes
aplazan
la suma de sus alas.
¿Vencer, quién vencerá?
Los copos
inician algaradas.
Sin ruido choques, nieves,
armiños, encontrados.
Pero el viento desata
deserciones, huidas,
y la que vence es
rosa, azul, sol, el alba:
punta de acero, pluma
contra lo blanco, en blanco,
inicial, tú, palabra.[7]

SHEET OF PAPER

Winter, the world in white.
Marbles, snow, feathers,
rain whiteness, build
whiteness, play whiteness.
Light as feathers,
illusive, tall columns
uphold roofs of white clouds.
Flights
of doves uncertain
between white above
and below, hesitant,
withhold
the whiteness of their wings.
Conquer, who will conquer?
The snowflakes
begin sudden attacks,
noiseless skirmishes, snows,
ermines, opposed.
But the wind, let loose,
brings flight, abandonment.
And that which conquers is
rose and blue, sun and dawn:

> point of steel, pen
> against the white, on white,
> you, the initial word.[8]

A mimetic reading of this poem, as a description of a winter landscape, is readily available to the reader. A critic might speculate on the verisimilar presence of ermines in such a scene, attempting to paint a coherent picture of clouds, columns, and doves. The Riffaterrian reading of the text, however, becomes obvious from the very beginning, with the repetition of *blanco* and *blancura* in the first four lines. The subtitle, "Cuartilla," indicates that the entire poem will consist of an extended metaphorical representation of the whiteness of the blank page. Mallarmé's "vide papier que la blancheur défend."[9] A *semiotic* reading, in Riffaterre's sense of the word, would explain *armiño* as the actualization of a literary paradigm, not as an animal literally present in the landscape. The best known such beast in Spanish poetry occurs in a sonnet of Góngora: "Salió el sol, y entre armiños escondida / soñolienta beldad con dulce saña / salteó el no bien sano pasajero."[10] [The sun came out, and, hidden among ermines / a sleepy beauty, with sweet cruelty / attacked the not so healthy traveller]. Góngora's ermines, like Salinas's, are associated with the arrival of dawn. In both poets the whiteness of this animal suggests the difficulty of distinguishing foreground from background: Salinas playfully transforms Góngora's "entre armiños escondida" into "armiños, encontrados."

The obvious nature of literary overdetermination in "Cuartilla" makes a Riffaterrian analysis appear unnecessary. The reader does not reject representation because of the lack of mimetic coherence—there are few overt "ungrammaticalities" here—but because the overdetermination of its semiotic code lies at the surface. The process by which the reader discovers the matrix ("whiteness"), and thus moves beyond the mimetic level, is short-circuited by the ease of the transition.[11] The central "ungrammaticality" in this text lies not in the referential incongruity of the ermines, but rather in the internal contradiction in the matrix of "whiteness": "contra lo blanco, en blanco." To paraphrase Riffaterre's paradigm, it is this ungrammaticality in the semiotic level that obliges us to search for a metasemiotic reading.

Critics have read "Cuartilla" as the depiction of a struggle between the white page and the poet's triumphant word. Julian Palley presents a more optimistic version of Mallarmé's struggle with the abyss of the white page: "Pero mientras Mallarmé nunca parece que emerge de su *néant*, de su *azur*, Salinas traba batalla continua con ella; y sus aliados en este encuentro son la palabra (el arte) y el amor" ["But while Mallarmé never seems to emerge from his *néant*, from his *azur*, Salinas undertakes a continual battle against it; and his allies in this encounter are the word (art) and love"].[12] Andrew Debicki also reads this and other poems from *Seguro azar* in existentialist terms: "El arte de la poesía resulta un modo de contrarrestar los efectos del tiempo, encontrando valores permanentes entre lo transitorio del mundo y salvando al hombre de su angustia"[13] ["The art of poetry turns out to be a way of arresting the effects of time, finding permanent values amid the transitoriness of the world and saving man from his anguish"]. These interpretations reveal more about the critics' assumptions than about the text itself. In the first place, the critics tend to identify the poet as one of the contestants, or even the winner, in the struggle that is first mentioned in the rhetorical question posed midway through the poem: "¿Vencer, quién vencerá?" Yet it is the dawn, subsequently identified with the point of the pen, that achieves victory, not the poet himself. The speaker of the poem never protrays the writing of the poem as a personal triumph: he maintains an ironic distance from the "conflict." Similarly, the poet's alleged foe, the white page, is not presented as the existential nothingness, complete with the ravages of time and man's anguish, that appears in the critics' readings.[14] The existentialist tone of the commentaries contrasts with the more detached, playful spirit of the poem: there is no explicit indication that the whiteness should be perceived as a threat to the poet's existence, or identified with any ethically negative idea.

The hypothesis that "Cuartilla" portrays the triumph of the poet's language over the blank page comes up against a final obstacle, for the marks made on the white page are, paradoxically, as white as the page itself: "contra lo blanco, en blanco." The writing is itself white, and thus as invisible against the whiteness of the page as a "polar bear in a snow storm." In this respect the victorious emergence of an apparently multicolored sunrise—"rosa, azul, sol, el alba"—is deceptive. A rosy pink, of course, is the traditional color of the dawn in Western literature from Homer onward; the blue is obviously that of the sky. These colors, however, are summarized in a word that negates their differentiation: *alba*, which etymologically is a synonym of *white*. The word shares the assonantal pattern of *blanca*, which culminates in the phonetically "white" word *palabra*. Salinas's poem retraces an act of poetic revelation in which the page's whiteness itself is revealed. Since the poem ends with the coming of dawn, the entire poem could be read as the white unveiling of whiteness. Paraphrasing the poem as an ironic description of a completely white canvas, one that negates all mimesis, the result is a "white dawn over snowy landscape of marble temples, clouds, doves, and ermines." The semiotic matrix of the text is not simply whiteness, however, but "white on white." Salinas's text explores the contradiction between light as the presence and as the absence of all color. The act of inscribing words on the page is not the triumph of meaning over meaninglessness, but the negative gesture of leaving the page as it is. Salinas writes with white ink, or with black ink that points to the white space surrounding it. In this respect he is a significant precursor of more recent Spanish poets such as Claudio Rodríguez and José Angel Valente, who view the act of poetic writing as a simultaneous negation and creation of meaning, a way of preserving the infinite possibilities of signification through an exploitation of poetic silence.

A metasemiotic reading of Salinas's "Cuartilla" is consistent both with Salinas's poetry as a whole and with the literary period in which he was writing.[15] Virtually every poem in *Seguro azar* comments upon the process of writing. Salinas's novel use of modern technology—light bulbs, cinemas, typewriters—serves to emphasize the artificial, antimimetic nature of poetic language. It has been noted that the last poem in the book, "Triunfo suyo" ["His triumph"] ends in silence, as opposed to "Cuartilla," which ends with the emergence of the word:

> Voy a verle cara a cara:
> porque ya se está quitando,
> porque está tirando ya
> los cielos, las alegrías,
> los disimulos, los tiempos,

las palabras, antifaces
leves que yo le ponía
contra—¡irresistible luz!—
su rostro de sin remedio
eternidad, él, silencio.

(*Poesías completas*, 162)

I shall see him face to face:
because already he is shedding,
already he is casting away,
heavens, joys, dissimulations,
times, words, the slight masks
under which I had hidden him
—irresistible light—
countenance of unavoidable eternity,
he, silence![16]

This apparent antithesis between language and silence, however, does not take into account the essentially silent nature of the poetic word. The triumph of silence at the conclusion of *Seguro azar* is anticipated from the very beginning, for the initial word unveiled in "Cuartilla" exemplifies a poetic language that does not disturb the silence of the blank page. The inscription of words on the page is, paradoxically, a prolongation of the blank moment that precedes writing.

Within the context of postsymbolist European poetry of the 1920s Salinas's self-consciousness is more typical than it is anomalous. (Self-conscious fiction, of which Salinas's own *Víspera del gozo* [Eve of delight] is a prominent example, also flourishes in the 1920s.) Philip Silver has suggested that Salinas's early poetry is best explained as a response to Vicente Huidobro's "creacionismo," the avant-garde doctrine that rejected *mimesis* in favor of *poesis*.[17] Although this is a plausible hypothesis, I prefer to trace Salinas's self-reflexive bent directly to his engagement with the French symbolist movement. Silver himself notes that Salinas was a sophisticated reader of Mallarmé.[18] Huidobro's "creationism" is essentially a rephrasing of the romantic notion that the writing of poetry is analogous to the creation of the world—rather than an imitation of what has already been created. In its crude dichotomies between creation and imitation, originality and derivativeness, Huidobro's theory would have offered Salinas much less food for thought than Mallarmé's more profound meditation on language.

Salinas's link to symbolist poetry leads us back to Riffaterre's theory of poetic semiotics, which is developed through analyses of nineteenth- and twentieth-century French poems. In light of Salinas's "Cuartilla," it is possible to read Riffaterre's own examples of poetic overdetermination thematically, that is, as self-conscious commentaries on the mimetic emptiness of poetic language, the absence of meaning that corresponds to a semiotic redundancy. It is striking how often Riffaterre's own examples explicitly thematize the *absence* of sense that he sees as the essence of poetic signification. The paradigm for this self-conscious anti-mimeticism is Mallarmé's notoriously hermetic "sonnet in -*yx*." Riffaterre perceptively views this text as a negation of mimesis. Mallarmé's "aboli bibelot d'inanité sonore," however, does not simply exemplify literary overdetermination, but also comments upon it directly: what is this "abolished knickknack of inane sonority" but the poem itself, which has been emptied of its mimetic meaning through the process of poetic semiosis? Mallarmé's struggle with the blank page, like Salinas's, is not a simple case of writer's block, but a sustained meditation on the semiotic "emptiness" of poetic language.

The preceding analysis of Salinas's "Cuartilla" reveals the strengths as well as the limitations of Riffaterre's *Semiotics of Poetry*. In the first place, Riffaterre's choice of texts is more historically contingent than he admits: his predilection for the modern period responds to the widespread concern with semiotic concerns among modern poets themselves.[19] Secondly, although Riffaterre attempts to maintain a separation between his own discourse and that of the poetic texts he analyzes, his theory is itself the product of developments in modern poetics from romanticism and symbolism onward. His theory rests on the dichotomy between literary and nonliterary language: "The language of poetry differs from common linguistic usage—this the most unsophisticated reader senses instinctively."[20] This distinction between literary language and ordinary language is, of course, one of the fundamental tenets of symbolist poetics. In this way the preoccupations of modern poets anticipate those of the theorist, since the poems analyzed in *Semiotics of Poetry* are already commentaries on the semiotic process that he elucidates. In spite of its neglect of the metasemiotic dimension of the poetic text, Riffaterre's theory is perhaps most useful as a theory of modern poetry, which self-consciously reflects upon the blankness of its own language.

II. The Mirror as Sign

A mirror image is not a sign, argues Umberto Eco.[21] Nevertheless, the mirror is the archetypal poetic metaphor for the relation of language to reality, probably because it stands at "the threshold between perception and signification."[22] Salinas's poetry often posits a specular relation between words and things. The lover-poet from *Presagios* through *Razón de amor* views his beloved *per speculum in aenigmate*. The mirror topos occurs early in Salinas's career. A poem from *Presagios* [Portents] (1923), his first volume, employs the same paradigm that governs the speaker's vision in the later love poetry of *La voz a ti debida* [My voice in debt to you]:

> ¡Cuánto rato te he mirado
> sin mirarte a ti, en la imagen
> exacta e inaccesible
> que te traiciona el espejo!
>
> *(Poesías completas, 60)*

> How long have I gazed at you
> without gazing at you, in the image—
> exact and inaccessible—
> by which the mirror betrays you!

One of the fundamental reasons that mirrors do not produce signs, according to Eco, is that they cannot be used to lie. True signs function autonomously, without the presence of the referent. Eco equates the mirror with prosthetic devices such as microscopes and telescopes, which are extensions of sense organs rather than vehicles for transmitting signs. Salinas, however, does posit a semiotics of the mirror: the reflection does not merely copy the referent, but rather simultaneously adds to and subtracts from it. The phrase "te traiciona el espejo" plays on ambiguity in the concept of *betrayal*, which could be defined as a morally dishonest act of revealing the truth. The proverbial truthfulness of the mirror, its incapacity to lie, serves a paradoxically deceitful purpose.

By preferring the mirror image over the woman herself, Salinas upsets the habitual hierarchy that places reality above its secondary representations:

> "Bésame", dices. Te beso,
> y mientras te beso pienso
> en lo fríos que serán
> tus labios en el espejo.
>
> (*Poesías completas*, 60)

> "Kiss me," you say. I kiss you
> and while I kiss you I think
> how cold your lips
> would be in the mirror.

The speaker of the poem, oddly enough, is distracted by the thought of the mirror image of the woman he is kissing. This thought leads to the characteristic Salinas paradox of *difficult ease*, also found in another poem from *Presagios:*

> El alma tenías
> tan clara y abierta
> que yo nunca pude
> entrarme en tu alma.
>
> (67)

> Your soul was
> so clear and open
> that I could never
> enter your soul.

In both poems the assonantal rhyme returns repeatedly to the same word, *espejo* and *alma* respectively. In both cases this tautological rhyme mirrors the speaker's obsessive complication of a search for a manifest truth that lies before his very eyes:

> "Toda el alma para ti",
> murmuras, pero en el pecho
> siento un vacío que sólo
> me lo llenará ese alma

que no me das.
El alma que se recata
con disfraz de claridades
en tu forma de espejo.

(*Poesías completas*, 60)

"All my soul is yours,"
you murmur, but in my chest
I feel an emptiness that only
will be filled by that soul
you don't give me.
The soul that hides
under a mask of clarities
in your shape in the mirror.

This conclusion willfully introduces obstacles to the mimetic directness of the mirror image, which is so immediate a representation of reality that it is not even semiotic in the technical sense. Salinas exploits the possible falseness of the mirror, a falseness which is itself the result of a trompe l'oeil illusion: the mirror is only deceptive if the viewer literally confuses it with reality, imagining a world behind the mirror. Even the apparent inversion of left and right is the product of our own perception rather than the mirror's duplicity. A reflection is so direct, according to Eco, that it does not know to invert left and right so as to return us our own image as others see us. Eco points out that the ability to use the mirror image—to comb one's hair for instance—implies the realization that the world behind the mirror is not real, that it is not possible to go through the looking glass with Alice.

The confusion between reality and its mirror image in Salinas's text evokes the myth of the handsome Greek youth who attempted to embrace his own reflected image. Although "narcissism" has come to connote an infatuation with one's self, the mythological Narcissus is unable to recognize his reflection for what it is. Mistaking an optical illusion for another person, he remains blind to his own self love. Salinas displaces and complicates this narcissistic self-embrace by introducing the woman into the reflected image. The kiss is double, taking place simultaneously on both sides of the mirror, with two Narcissus and two Echo figures. At the same time, he repeats Narcissus's explicit flight from the feminine, preferring to imagine a colder, desexualized encounter with his companion. His consciousness of the unreality of the world through the looking glass remains halfway between Narcissus's blindness and Umberto Eco's metasemiotic lucidity.

"Para cristal te quiero," from *Seguro azar*, presents another perspective on the mirror. In this case the poet attempts to escape from narcissism:

AMIGA

Para cristal te quiero
nítida y clara eres.
Para mirar el mundo,
a través de ti, puro,
de hollín o de belleza,
como lo invente el día.
Tu presencia aquí, sí,
delante de mí, siempre,
pero invisible siempre,
sin verte y verdadera.
Cristal. ¡espejo nunca!

(*Poesías completas*, 159)

FRIEND

Like crystal I want you
so sharp and clear you are.
To see the world
through you: pure,
made of soot or of beauty
the way the day invents it.
Your presence here, yes,
before me always,
but invisible always—
without seeing yourself—and true.
Crystal. Never a mirror!

As in "Cuartilla," Salinas uses the parenthetical subtitle to name the object of metaphorical comparison. Here the metaphor cuts both ways: the crystal pane is a metaphor for the woman's transparency, and the woman in turn represents an ideal artistic transparency. She is not the object of the poet's gaze, but rather a metaphor for the purity and transparency of the artistic medium. As Claudio Rodríguez has put it in a similar poem:

Quisiera estar contigo no por verte
sino por ver lo mismo que tú, cada
cosa en la que respiras como en esta
lluvia de tanta sencillez, que lava.[23]

I want to be with you not to see you
but to see the same as you, each
thing in which you breathe as in this
rain, so simple, which washes.

Much of Salinas's poetry presents a paradoxical image of the woman as an immanent presence, immediately available for comprehension, and an evasive absence. Her immanence becomes unfathomable because of the complexity of the poet's masculine mind. In this poem, however, the poet glimpses the possibilities of a more directly transparent poetic language in which he can leave behind his overly complicated specularity.

The paradigm developed in "Cuánto rato" is more frequent in Salinas's work than the counterexample of "Para cristal te quiero." Poem 52 of Salinas's best-known sequence, *La voz a ti debida*, is a further elaboration of this paradigm:

Distánciamela, espejo;
trastorna su tamaño.
A ella, que llena el mundo,
hazla menuda, mínima.
Que quepa en monosílabos,
en unos ojos;
que la puedas tener
a ella, desmesurada,
gacela, ya sujeta,
infantil, en tu marco.
Quítale esa delicia
del ardor y del bulto,
que no la sientan ya
las últimas balanzas;
déjala fría, lisa,
enterrada en tu azogue.
Desvía
su mirada; que no
me vea, que se crea
que está sola.
Que yo sepa, por fin,
cómo es cuando esté sola.

Entrégame tú de ella
lo que no me dio nunca.

Aunque así
—¡Qué verdad revelada!—
aunque así, me la quites.

(*Poesías completas*, 302)

Distance her from me, mirror;
disturb her size.
Take her, who fills the world,
and make her tiny, minimal.
Let her fit in monosyllables,
in someone's eyes;
so that you can hold her—
like a gazelle, already tame—
childlike in your frame.
Take from her that delight
of her heat and her mass
so that the last scales
no longer feel her weight;
leave her cold, smooth,
buried in your quicksilver.
Divert
her gaze; so she won't
see me, so she'll think
she's alone.
Let me know, finally,
What she's like when she's alone.
Give me that part of her
that she never gave me.

Even though—
what truth is revealed—
even though you thus take her away from me.

Salinas's tendency to reduce and distance, and even to murder,
his beloved comes to the forefront in this text. Language, represented here by its most minimal elements ("monosílabos"), shares
the mirror's capacity to transform living reality into a lifeless essence. By addressing the mirror directly, rather than the woman
whose body is reduced, the poetic voice self-consciously emphasizes the medium of representation—at the expense of the reality
represented.

A complete reading of this poem, however, must take into account the last three lines, which expose the preceding twenty-four as a defensive strategy. The poet-lover deliberately chooses the woman's inner truth—supposedly revealed in the mirror image—over her vital presence; even at the risk of losing her, he reduces her to a timeless essence. Yet his reductionism also serves to insulate him against the certainty of his loss. This loss is not a risk that he assumes, but rather the symbolic action that his words effect. This concluding note of pathos distinguishes the poem from the more playful tone of "Cuánto rato." "Distáncia-mela," then, inverts the poet's preference for the coldness of the mirror over the warmth of another human being. The text becomes a poignant mirror image or a photographic negative of the presence it purposefully renounces. As others have pointed out, *La voz a ti debida* tells the story of a love affair. But the poet is haunted by a sense of loss from the very beginning.[24] His desire to essentialize the woman through the linguistic mirror of poetry stems from his hopelessness in the face of her living reality.

Many critics have described the poetry of Guillén, Salinas, and other poets of the 1920s in terms of a loosely defined "pure poetry." Cano Ballesta and Blanch, for example, use the term to designate a period style, without reflecting upon its theoretical implications.[25] Many simply affirm, tautologically, the idea that pure poetry eliminates supposedly "impure" elements such as politics, narration, didacticism, and excessive sentimentality. Yet if pure poetry reduces poetry to its pure elements, what precisely are these elements? The preceding consideration of Salinas's semiotics of poetry leads to a more specific answer to this question. His "pure poetry" is a purification of language as a semiotic medium; its principal aim is to attenuate the referentiality of poetic language. In its self-conscious representations of writing—the blank page and the mirror—Salinas's poetry reflects upon the process of this poetic semiosis.

3

Vicente Aleixandre: "Límites y espejo"

The image of Vicente Aleixandre as a relatively unsophisticated creator has been remarkably tenacious, although no one has ever called into question his mastery of language. The stylistic analyses of Carlos Bousoño, the author of the first and most influential monograph on the poet, have provided ample demonstration of the subtlety and power of Aleixandre's poetic technique. Still, few studies of his poetry have emphasized his linguistic self-consciousness, his awareness of the verbal medium as a theoretical problem.[1] In a recent study, Philip Silver has given voice to the widespread view that Aleixandre is essentially naive as a poetic thinker. For Silver, the author of *La destrucción o el amor* typifies the Hispanic poet who, like Antaeus in Greek mythology, derives all of his strength from his ties to the earth.[2] Aleixandre would thus lack the theoretical self-consciousness that is essential to the modern poet.

This assessment, I would argue, makes the poet a victim of his own rhetoric. Many of Aleixandre's statements about his own work give the initial impression of a resolutely antitheoretical poet, more concerned with the content of his poetic vision than with language per se. In a statement of his poetics written in the 1930s for Gerardo Diego's anthology, for example, he protests against what he perceives to be a widespread tendency in modern poetry to exalt language for its own sake: "Frente a la divinización de la palabra, frente a esa casi obscena delectación de la *Maestría* o dominio verbal del artífice que trabaja la talla, confundiendo el destello del vidrio entre sus manos con la profunda luz creadora, hay que afirmar, hay que exclamar con verdad. No, la poesía no es *cuestión de palabras*" [In opposition to the deification of the word, to that almost obscene pleasure in the *mastery* or verbal skill of the artificer who fabricates his sculpture, confusing the gleam of glass in his hands with the profound creative light, it is necessary to affirm, to exclaim truthfully. No, poetry is not *a question of words*:].[3]

Aleixandre appears to be exalting the content of the poet's vision at the expense of a concern for the verbal medium itself. He rejects the notion that the poet is primarily a wordsmith, refining language into a more perfect medium for the expression of thought.[4] It could be argued, however, that Aleixandre's apparent denial of the linguistic nature of poetry reveals an obsession with language. His very distrust of words obliges him to consider the question of language in a way that a more obviously logophilic poet would not. I would argue that his attitude of suspicion is more characteristic of the modern poet than is the simple exaltation of poetic language. Aleixandre's poetry is indeed a "question of words," in the sense that it is both a quest for expression and a questioning of language. In his profession of the primacy of experience over words, Aleixandre aligns himself with one of the central currents of poetry since romanticism, the tradition that views language as an inherently defective system of signs that must continually be destroyed and recreated. Octavio Paz has succinctly summarized this attitude toward language in terms of a double imperative: "a un tiempo, destrucción y creación del lenguaje. Destrucción de las palabras y de los significados, reino del silencio; pero, igualmente, palabra en busca de la Palabra." ["At once a destruction and a creation of language. A destruction of words and of signifieds, a realm of silence; but, equally, a word in search of the Word"].[5]

While adamantly denying that it is a question of words, Aleixandre concludes his statement by defining poetry in terms of language. He dismisses everyday words as "estrechos moldes previos" ["narrow, preestablished molds"] and "signos insuficientes" ["insufficient signs"] from which the poetic genius must escape:

> fuga o destino hacia un generoso reino, plenitud o realidad soberana, realidad suprasensible, mundo incierto donde el enigma de la poesía está atravesado por las supremas categorías, últimas potencias que iluminan y signan la oscura revelación para la que las palabras trastornan su consuetudinario sentido.
>
> (*Obras completas* 2:645)

a flight or a destiny toward a generous realm, a plenitude or sovereign reality, a reality superior to the senses, an uncertain world where the enigma of poetry is transfixed by supreme categories, ultimate powers that illuminate and seal that dark revelation for the sake of which words disturb their everyday sense.

Although the poet emphasizes the reality that lies beyond ordinary perception and ordinary language, this marvelous realm can be reached only through a specifically verbal act: the subversion of the accepted usage of words. This disturbance of sense implies the creation of a new and paradoxical poetic speech, one that will somehow correspond to the dark revelation, the paradoxically opaque unveiling, of poetic vision.

It has been customary to divide Aleixandre's poetic production into three major periods: the early surrealist-influenced poetry, the "realist" tendency of the postwar period, and the metaphysical investigations of *Poemas de la consumación* [Poems of consummation] (1968) and *Diálogos del conocimiento* [Dialogues of knowledge] (1974). Aleixandre's self-consciousness is most evident at the beginning and at the end of his long career. In many poems written during the 1930s, the poet expresses his view of language in terms very similar to those he employs in his *poética*. Words in their ordinary state impede the poet's expression of his vision, or even his access to it. In a poem from *Espadas como labios* [Swords like lips] (1932), "Palabras," the speaker views language in essentially negative terms:

> Pero no importa que todo esté tranquilo
> (La palabra esa lana marchita)
> Flor tú muchacha casi desnuda viva viva
> (la palabra esa arena machacada)[6]

> But it doesn't matter that everything is calm
> (The word that faded wool)
> Flower you girl almost naked alive alive
> (the word that pounded sand)

Once again, this denigration of words must be understood as part of a dialectical movement. Language is an obstacle to expression, but a necessary one, for without its interference or resistance there would be no tension between the words of the poem and the reality that they attempt to capture.

It could be argued that it is the tension between the poet's vision and its linguistic expression, rather than content of his vision per se, that most preoccupies the early Aleixandre. Paul Ilie, for example, has convincingly interpreted *Pasión de la tierra* [Passion of the earth] as an allegory of the poet's anxiety about his poetic gift.[7] The opening poem of *Espadas como labios*, entitled "Mi voz," calls into question virtually every aspect of the communicative situation:

He nacido una noche de verano
entre dos pausas Háblame te escucho
He nacido Si vieras qué agonía
representa la luna sin esfuerzo
He nacido Tu nombre era la dicha
Bajo un fulgor una esperanza un ave
Llegar llegar El mar era un latido
el hueco de una mano una medalla tibia
Entonces son posibles ya las luces las caricias la piel el horizonte
ese decir palabras sin sentido
que ruedan como oídos caracoles
como un lóbulo abierto que amanece
(escucha escucha) entre la luz pisada[8]

I have been born one summer's night
between two pauses Speak to me I listen to you
I have been born If you could see what agony
the moon effortlessly represents
I have been born Your name was joy
Beneath a brilliance a hope a bird
To arrive to arrive The sea was a heartbeat
the hollow of a hand a warm medal
Then the lights the caresses the skin the horizon become possible
that speaking of senseless words
that roll like ears snails
like an open lobe that dawns
(listen listen) amid the trampled light

In his landmark essay "Closing Statement: Linguistics and Poetics," Roman Jakobson posited a model of communication consisting of six elements: addressor, addressee, contact, code, message, and context. According to Jakobson, different kinds of utterances privilege one or another of six functions.[9] In Aleixandre's text, however, none of these elements is fully functional. The lyric speaker and his addressee—two isolated and vaguely defined personages—seem unable to establish contact with each other. Nor do they share any meaningful code, striving only to "decir palabras sin sentido." As in much modern poetry, the referential function (for Jakobson, a focus on the context of utterance) is extremely weak. Of course, the text constitutes a "poetic" use of language, in that it focuses on the message for its own sake. Yet, because of the weakness of the other five elements, this poetic function has the effect of undermining rather than contributing to the act of communication.

It is interesting to note that Aleixandre's critics have tended to privilege *La destrucción o el amor* [Destruction or love], which contains fewer explicitly self-conscious poems, over *Pasión de la tierra* and *Espadas como labios,* his two earlier surrealist works. The poetic voice heard in this volume appears to be more confident of its communicative power, as Aleixandre develops a more powerful but also more predictable set of rhetorical devices. The resulting confidence in language ultimately leads, in Aleixandre's second period, to a very different kind of metapoetry. Words continue to be perceived as obstacles to the attainment of poetic vision. The most significant novelty in the books written during the forties and fifties, however, is that this linguistic interference is much more easily displaced. A relative clarity of expression replaces the tortured struggle with language characteristic of the earlier poetry. In a passage notable for its magnificent rhetoric, the speaker of "El poeta," the initial poem in *Sombra del paraíso* [Shadow of paradise])1944), instructs the poet who is about to read the book to throw it down, to reject it as an inadequate representation of the vitality of nature:

> Sí, poeta, arroja este libro que pretende encerrar en sus páginas un destello del sol,
> y mira a la luz cara a cara, apoyada la cabeza en la roca,
> mientras tus pies remotísimos sienten el beso postrero del poniente
> y tus manos alzadas tocan dulce la luna,
> y tu cabellera colgante deja estela en los astros.
>
> (*Obras completas,* 1:484)

> Yes, poet, throw down this book which claims to enclose in its pages a glimmer of sunlight,

and look at the light face to face, with your head resting on a rock,
while your remote feet feel the last kiss of the west wind
and your raised hands touch the sweet moon,
and your hair, hanging down, leaves its wake among the stars.

The obvious paradox here is that these words do not have the effect of prompting the lyric addressee (or the real reader, for that matter) to stop reading the book. The result is likely to be exactly the opposite: the speaker's words create the illusion that the book in question is not really a text at all, but an unmediated encounter with the naked elements of Aleixandre's paradise.[10] This passage contains an implicit message to its readers instructing them to ignore the linguistic medium of poetry, to look through the language as though it were a transparent glass that allowed them to come face to face with the light of the poet's transcendent vision.

The books that follow *Sombra del paraíso* continue to elide the question of language. In *Historia del corazón* [History of the heart] (1954) and *En un vasto dominio* [In a vast dominion] (1962) Aleixandre no longer rejects everyday language as an impediment to a transcendent poetic vision. Rather, he accepts this language as an unproblematic channel of communication. Reading these books, one no longer senses any tension between language and its referents. The poet's lack of interest in poetic language as a problem corresponds to his desire to reach the largest possible audience. In the manifesto-like poem that opens *En un vasto dominio* [In a vast domain], "¿Para quién escribo?" [For whom do I write?] (*Obras completas*, 1:797–99), the speaker affirms that his goal is to give voice to the concerns of those who cannot speak. For such a poetics, diametrically opposed to that of *Espadas como labios*, language is no longer a problem or even a question. It becomes a mere tool for the expression of meaning. If the poet is not a goldsmith he is at least a blacksmith. What the Aleixandre of these years shares with the poet who conceives of his craft as fine metalwork is a certain complacency about the capacity of language to obey his will, to represent his vision of reality unproblematically.

In the final phase of his career Aleixandre returns to a more complex vision of language, one that is reminiscent to some degree of his earlier poetics. Aleixandre's renewed interest in metapoetry corresponds to a widespread awakening of self-consciousness in Spanish poetry of the sixties and seventies. Led by young poets such as Guillermo Carnero and Pere Gimferrer, poets of all generations and tendencies begin to call language into question with renewed fervor. It is no coincidence that Aleixandre is one of the major sponsors of these younger poets, or that Carnero and Gimferrer have both written intelligently and sympathetically about Aleixandre's later work.

Poemas de la consumación, like Espadas como labios, Sombra del paraíso, and En un vasto dominio, begins with a statement of poetics. "Las palabras del poeta" ["The poet's words"], however, is an elusive text, far from the programmatic statement of intentions of "Para quién escribo."[11] The poetic voice here is neither the vital, Whitmanesque singer of the former poem nor the Great Communicator of the latter. He is instead an old man whose words begin to fail him in the face of his impending end. At this point in the poet's career the mediation of words cannot be side-stepped: words are no longer direct representations of an available reality, as in Aleixandre's "realist" phase, but a medium for the preservation of memory:

Después de la palabras muertas,
de las aún pronunciadas o dichas,
¿qué esperas? Unas hojas volantes,
más papeles dispersos. ¿Quién sabe? Unas palabras
deshechas, como el eco o la luz que muere allá en gran noche.
                                        (Obras completas, 2:31)

After the dead words,
those already pronounced or spoken,
what do you expect? Some flying leaves,
more dispersed papers. Who knows? Some words
undone, like the echo or the light that dies there in the great night.

This poem sets forward in discursive terms the implicit poetics of Poemas de la consumación. Language is no longer a transparent medium that can bring the poet and his readers into direct contact with a poetic vision of reality. Instead, it is an echo, a belated representation. As in both Aleixandre's early and middle periods, there is an implicit opposition between language and vitality. Here, however, the poet no longer has any access to this vitality outside of language. As a consequence, language is paradoxically identified with as well as opposed to life: "Morir es olvidar unas palabras" ["To die is to forget some words"].

While only a half-dozen poems after "Las palabras del poeta" explicitly address the linguistic theme, virtually all the poems in the volume touch upon it in some way. The structure of *Poemas de la consumación* allows a metapoetic reading of many poems that otherwise might not lend themselves to this approach. As with all of his books of poetry, with the exception of a few anthologies and miscellanies, Aleixandre has conceived the volume as an interdependent group of closely related poems, rather than a mere agglomeration of lyric poems. If anything, the book is even more tightly knit than the poet's previous efforts. For Gimferrer, Aleixandre's later poetry is "un arte combinatorio que procede por permutación, sustitución o superposición de un repertorio muy parco de elementos" ["An *ars combinatoria* that proceeds by permutation, substitution, or superposition of a very limited repertory of elements"].[12] Gimferrer goes on to make the surprising affirmation that the reiterative and paradigmatic structure of these books is imperceptible to the common reader, emerging only from the critic's analysis. I would argue, on the contrary, that this distinction is arbitrary, and that an awareness of the repetition of basic elements is an indispensable part of any reader's experience of the text. It is only by comparing and contrasting individual poems that one constructs a paradigm and thus makes sense of the larger whole. The "common reader" is a mere fiction in this case, given the already small audience for poetry and the difficulty of Aleixandre's final works.

Since terms that relate to language specifically and to representation in general have a crucial place within the densely woven semantic web of the book, it is not necessary or even desirable to concentrate exclusively on the poet's more explicit statements of poetics. I would begin charting the semantic system of *Poemas de la consumación* with the key word *palabra* [word], which relates directly to other types of signs—*signos, emblemas, nombres, textos* [signs, emblems, names, texts]—and to words that refer literally or metaphorically to poetry: *poeta, palabra, canción* [poet, word, song]. *Palabra* is also linked to words pertaining to orality: *voz, boca, beso, lengua, labios* [voice, mouth, kiss, tongue (or language), lips]. A line such as "roja pulpa besada que pronuncian" ["red kissed pulp that they pronounce"] (*Obras completas*, 2:73) conflates the speech-act and the kiss, so that the word becomes an explicitly erotic act. There is another set of terms having to do with sound: *son, sonido, eco, silencio, callar* [sound, echo, silence, to quiet]. Moving in another direction, language is linked metaphorically to other belated representations of reality: *espejo, imagen, reflejo, copia, sombra, huella, repetir* [mirror, image, reflection, copy, shadow, trace, to repeat]. The imperfection of linguistic representation finds expression in words such as *engaño, máscara, mentira, verdad, sueño* [deceit, mask, lie, truth, dream]. These terms lead us directly to the problem of knowledge that Guillermo Carnero has studied in Aleixandre's later work.[13] This epistemological preoccupation is often expressed in imagery of light and darkness: *luz, oscuridad, mirar, ciego, ver, saber, conocer* [light, darkness, to look, blind, to see, to know, to be familiar with].

These chains of words could be extended into a complete glossary of the significant terms that appear in *Poemas*. The result of Aleixandre's technique is an implicit mode of poetic self-reflection that has not been widely appreciated. In order to demonstrate how this implicit self-consciousness functions in *Poemas de la consumación*, I have chosen to analyze a representative poem, "Límites y espejo" [Limits and mirror], which, aside from the presence of the word *palabras*, is not one of the half-dozen or so that explicitly address the question of the poet's language.

The same semantic structure that makes it difficult to interpret a single poem as an independent unit also allows such a poem to be representative of the larger whole. The opening lines of "Límites y espejo," in the context of the volume as a whole, take on intertextual resonance. The abrupt way in which the poem begins, with a command to an unnamed interlocutor, implies the continuation of a previous dialogue. The enigmatic, aphoristic style and the brevity of the text, similarly, encourage the reader to look for help in the other poems in the book.

> No insistas. La juventud no engaña. Brilla a solas.
> En un pecho desnudo muere el día.
> No son palabras las que a mí me engañan.
> Sino el silencio puro que aquí nace.

En tus bordes. La silenciosa línea te limita
pero no te reduce. Oh, tu verdad latiendo aquí en espacios.
                                              (*Obras completas*, 2:74)

Don't insist. Youth does not deceive. It shines alone.
In a naked chest the day dies.
What deceives me is not words.
But the pure silence that is born here.
On your edges. The silent line delimits you.
But doesn't reduce you. Oh, your truth beating here in spaces.

The first four lines recombine elements from the beginnings of
the poems that immediately precede it in section 4 of the book:
"La juventud engaña / con veraces palabras" ["Youth deceives /
with true words"] (2:71). "Felicidad, no engañas. / Una palabra
fue o sería, y dulce / quedó en el labio ["Happiness, you don't
deceive. / It was or would be a word, and sweetly / it stayed on
my lip"] (2:72). "La juventud no lo conoce, por eso dura, y sigue"
["Youth does not know it, and because of this it lasts, and continues"] (2:73). These poems, variations on a theme, evoke two semantic networks: language and its deceptiveness, and the
contrast between youth and old age that the majority of critics
have seen as the major theme of Aleixandre's later poetry. "Límites
y espejo" is a representative poem in *Poemas de la consumación*
because of the way in which it fuses these two preoccupations.
My thesis is that Aleixandre views the opposition between youth
and old age in terms of a parallel opposition between reality and
its imperfect linguistic representation. Old age is a pallid reflection of youth, just as language echoes but does not capture what
it attempts to represent. The title of the poem, in this case, would
suggest the *limits* of language's *mirroring*, which has the paradoxical effect of imitating reality while missing the essential truth.

Limits and borders in Aleixandre's poetry almost always have
an ambiguous meaning. By definition they circumscribe and de-
limit. At the same time, to reach the limit is to come into contact
with the absolute. The lover in *La destrucción o el amor*, for example,
feels "los hermosos límites de la vida" [the beautiful limits of life]
(1:331). In the mirror's visual image, the poet attempts to have the
benefits of mimesis without its drawbacks. He wishes to create a
representation that limits without being reductive. The line, by
defining the outlines of the image, also gives it its human, mortal

dimension, and thus defines its essential truth. The "pure silence" of vision would appear to transcend the inherent deceptiveness of language. The mirror, of course, is a traditional symbol of pure, unmediated mimesis, though it can also represent the dangers of such mimesis, as in the myth of Narcissus. The second-person singular *tú* in these lines could be seen as a double of the poet. I would interpret this figure, however, as the poet's younger beloved, who appears in other poems of the volume. This female figure would thus stand in contrast to the older poet, who remains trapped within the less perfect medium of language.

The second stanza of "Límites y espejo" links the ambiguity of limits to another, similar paradox having to do with consummation, perfection, and death:

> Sólo un cuerpo desnudo enseña bordes.
> Quien se limita existe. Tú en la tierra.
> Cuán diferente tierra se descoge
> y se agrupa y reluce y, suma, enciéndese,
> carne o resina, o cuerpo, alto, latiendo,
> llameando. Oh, si vivir es consumirse, ¡muere!

> Only a naked body shows edges.
> He who limits himself exists. You on the earth.
> What a different earth unfolds
> and regroups and shines and, a summation, is lit,
> flesh or resin, or a high body, beating,
> flaming. Oh, if to live is to be consumed, die!

Consumación means "fulfillment, consummation, perfection." In Spanish, however, the word has the secondary meaning of "extinction, death, the end of time." Thus it combines the connotations of two distinct verbs, *consumar* and *consumir*. As the flame of life reaches its limits it consumes itself and at the same time reaches its point of consummation. This stanza describes the image of the beloved in the mirror in terms of Aleixandre's view of human life as a momentary state of exception in the universe. The limits are both spatial and temporal: they are the edges of her body, and the time frame that defines her existence as a "different kind of earth," one that only very briefly takes on human form. The brevity of life, its exceptionality in the context of the entire cosmos, is expressed in the virtual simultaneity of birth and death.[14] By emphasizing the shortness of the human life span, the poet is able to minimize the possible difference in age between the poet and his beloved: if birth and death occur together, like the beginning and end of a lightning bolt, youth and old age become practically indistinguishable.

The third and final stanza of the poem returns to the idea of the imperfection of representation, striking a more subdued tone after the exaltation of the second section:

Pero quien muere nace, y aquí aún existes.
¿La misma? No es un espejo un rostro aunque repita
su gesto. Quizá su voz. En el espejo hiélase una imagen
de un sonido. ¡Cómo en el vidrio el labio dejó huellas!
El vaho tan sólo de lo que tú amaras.

But the one who dies is born, and here you still exist.
The same woman? A face is not a mirror although it repeats
its expression. Perhaps her voice. In the mirror the sound of an
    image
is frozen. How the lip left traces on the glass!
Only the exhalation of what you had loved.

In contrast to the more optimistic tone of the beginning of the poem, the speaker now emphasizes the inadequacy of representation: a mirror is not the face it reflects. In the first stanza, the essential truth of the woman persists in the illusory three-dimensionality of the mirror's reflection ("Oh tu verdad latiendo aquí en espacios"). Now, however, the mirror freezes the reality that it reflects, converting even the poet's voice into an inert, spatial representation, twice removed from its source. The image of kissing the mirror calls to mind the lines from Pedro Salinas's *Presagios* analyzed in the previous chapter:

'Bésame', dices. Te beso,
y mientras te beso pienso
en lo fríos que serán
tus labios en el espejo.

The situation in Aleixandre's poem, however, is almost the exact reverse. Instead of kissing the woman while thinking of her reflection in the mirror, as does the speaker in the Salinas poem, Aleixandre's speaker conceives of his erotic encounter through the indirect medium of the mirror image. In the immediacy of the moment Salinas attempts to distance the kiss by converting it into a cold representation of itself. Aleixandre, in contrast, feels the last warmth of a past sexual union in the imprint of his lover's lips on the glass. We should remember that, in the semantic universe of *Poemas de la consumación*, kissing and speaking are often parallel acts. The poet, at the terminal point in his life, becomes the empty image of what his companion had loved.

The poem that immediately follows "Límites y espejo" in *Poemas de la consumación*, "Rostro tras el cristal (Mirada del viejo)" ["Face behind the pane (An old man's gaze)"] is another variation on the same theme:

> O tarde o pronto o nunca.
> Pero ahí tras el cristal el rostro insiste.
> Junto a unas flores naturales la misma flor se muestra
> en forma de color, mejilla, rosa.
> Tras el cristal la rosa es siempre rosa.
> Pero no huele.
> La juventud distante es ella misma.
> Pero aquí no se oye.
>
> Sólo la luz traspasa el cristal virgen.
>
> (Obras completas, 2:75)

> Later or sooner or never.
> But there behind the glass the face insists.
> Next to the natural flowers the same flower is revealed
> in form of color, cheek, rose.
> Behind the pane the rose is always a rose.
> But it has no odor.
> Distant, youth is itself,
> but here it can't be heard.
>
> Only light traverses the virgin crystal.

In this case a windowpane takes the place of the mirror. As in "Límites," the poem is structured around the contrast between youth and old age, sight and sound (and in this case smell), reality and its sensory representation. The poet observes his beloved through a medium that preserves her image in its purified form, while separating him from its vitality. Unlike "Límites y espejo," this poem does not explicitly mention language, "las palabras."

Nevertheless, it forms part of Aleixandre's overall meditation on the limits of representation, and thus exhibits the self-reflexivity that characterizes all of the poet's later work.

The term *metapoetry* usually implies the existence of another kind of poetry, one that does not reflect upon itself. The implicit mode of self-reflection found in Aleixandre's later work, however, subverts any line the critic might wish to draw between metapoetry and other modes of poetic discourse. Theories of poetic self-consciousness are often based on the idea of the subversion of mimesis. It might be argued, though, that mimesis is not a generic norm for lyric poetry in the same way it is for other genres. Unlike prose narration or theater, where the reader might expect to find an illusion of reality, poetry is already an inherently self-reflexive genre, one that rarely claims to be referential. Thus any attempt to distinguish between ordinary poetic discourse and the self-conscious commentary on this discourse will beg the question of what constitutes poetic language in the first place.

In Aleixandre's later poetry, the question of poetic language becomes inseparable from the epistemological problem of the relation between reality and its representation, and the vital problem posed by the imminence of old age and death. In *Poemas de la consumación* the limits of language come to represent the limits of life itself. Poetic language reflects upon itself in the act of representation, or, more accurately, in the process of failing to represent a more essential reality. This "failure" is the consummate achievement of Aleixandre's later poetry.

4

The Word Made Flesh: Logocentrism in the Later Work of José Angel Valente

Critics have repeatedly signaled the innovations introduced into postwar Spanish poetry by a group of groundbreaking young poets who came of age in the 1950s and reoriented contemporary Spanish poetry toward more aesthetic values in the wake of the "social poetry" of the earlier postwar years.[1] This chapter will consider the attitudes toward language of one of the most significant writers of this group, José Angel Valente (1929–). The focus will be on his later work, especially the important books published since 1980.[2] Chapters 5 and 6 will examine the poetry of Antonio Gamoneda and Jaime Gil de Biedma, two other poets of this period whose poetry and poetics can be fruitfully compared to those of Valente. Together, these three chapters aim to reevaluate some prevalent critical views of this important cohort of Spanish poets.

The poetry of the 1950s represents a reprise of the preoccupation with poetic language seen in the poets of the "Generation of 1927," as well as an anticipation of the exaggerated literary self-consciousness of the poets who begin to write in the late 1960s and early 1970s. Andrew Debicki has viewed both the Rodríguez–Valente group and these younger poets, commonly known as the *novísimos*, as postmodernists.[3] The *novísimos* do in fact take an unmistakably postmodern stance, which I shall attempt to define in chapter 7. The midcentury poets occupy a more ambiguous niche in literary history, since their postmodernism manifests itself in a less overt and self-conscious way. These poets generally show no salient interest in mass culture, and most would reject the explicit antihumanism of much French poststructuralism. As Debicki suggests, these writers do not go as far as some of the *novísimos* in questioning traditional notions of subjectivity: "Aunque desconfíen, en principio, de la inmutabilidad de la obra literaria, siguen tratando de encarnar en su poesía la esencia de su ser" [Although they distrust the immutability of the literary work in principle, they continue their attempts to incarnate in their poetry the essence of their being"].[4]

Valente and his contemporaries have been called *postmodern* primarily because of their skeptical attitude toward language. The notion of "linguistic skepticism" has been a fertile hypothesis. Critics have tended to contrast an earlier faith in language, exemplified by poets such as Jorge Guillén, with an increased distrust in the linguistic medium among younger poets.[5] This opposition rests on two broad generalizations. The first is the notion that modernism in Spain is a unified movement whose most typical exponent is Jorge Guillén. Guillén's philosophy of language, however, is considerably less "skeptical" than that of his contemporaries Pedro Salinas and Vicente Aleixandre. The view that the poets of the 1950s are more skeptical about the capacity of language to represent reality is open to question. The great emphasis placed on the indeterminacy of meaning in the work of these poets, I would contend, has obscured an equally crucial movement toward closure in their work.

Several critics have explored the various strategies that Valente employs to suggest the multiplicity of possible interpretations of his works.[6] His concept of "punto cero" exemplifies the ideal of semantic indeterminacy that is shared by several poets of the period: "La palabra ha de llevar el lenguaje al punto cero, al punto de la indeterminación infinita, de la infinita libertad" ["The word must take language to the zero point, to the point of maximum indetermination, of infinite freedom"] (*Punto cero*, 7). This indeterminacy principle is implicit in the views of the creative process prevalent among these writers. The poet does not have a preconceived idea of what he or she is going to say: the poem is discovered in the act of writing itself.

Without denying the skepticism and indeterminacy that critics have discerned in Valente's work, I would approach the problem in a somewhat different way. He is a "logocentric" poet in a literal sense, in that he places the *logos* at the center of his preoccupations. He does distrust inauthentic language, but at the same time his critique of such a language logically implies the existence of an authentic Word. His conception of poetic language is a fundamentally religious one, rooted in Christian (and specifically in Catholic) traditions. Peter Dunn explains the medieval view of the world as a book written by God:

> If the universe is a book in which we try to read God's intention, books written by mortal writers are mirrors of mirrors, containing reflections of reflections. One must believe God's signs to be stable, free from deceit, all pointing to him and his purpose for mankind. Man's signs, including his languages, are unstable; their indeterminacies, slippages, aporias, are simply evidence of our fallen nature, our alienation, cut off from both the world's beginning and its end.[7]

The skepticism shown toward language in the medieval worldview is not absolute, since the imperfection of human signs contrasts with the perfection of the divine Word. Although Valente ultimately questions this perfection, his attitude toward language rests on a similar dialectic. In the last analysis, his skeptical attitude only makes sense if one assumes the transcendence of language in the first place. Otherwise, a more utilitarian and less problematic view of words would replace the anguished search for a more authentic means of expression. In many of the same poems in which language is viewed as an obstacle to transcendence, language is also the only means of overcoming this obstacle. The opposition, in other words, is not between language and nonlinguistic reality, but between two sorts of language.

In "Como una invitación o una súplica" ["Like an invitation or a supplication"] from *La memoria y los signos* [Memory and signs], words are personified and given an autonomy from the human agents who use them. As the poem opens, the speaker complains of established combinations of words that perpetuate outworn habits and ideas and thus frustrate the search for an authentic poetic language:

> Bajo la palabra insistente
> como una invitación o una súplica
> debíamos hallarnos, debíamos hallar
> una brizna de mundo.

Pero las palabras se unían
formando frases
y las frases se unían a sus ritmos antiguos:
los ritmos componían
el son inútil de la letra muerta
y de la vieja moralidad.

(*Punto cero*, 229)

Beneath the insistent word
like an invitation or a supplication
we should have found ourselves, we should have found
a shred of world.

But the words joined together
forming sentences
and the sentences joined their old rhythms:
the rhythms formed
the useless sound of the dead letter
and of the old morality.

The phrase "letra muerta" implicitly evokes its opposite, the notion of the living spirit that is absent from habitual combinations of words. This worn-out medium calls for a Mallarméan purification at the hands of the poet:

En vano vuelven las palabras
pues ellas mismas todavía esperan
la mano que las quiebre y las vacíe
hasta hacerlas ininteligibles y puras
para que de ellas nazca un sentido distinto,
incomprensible y claro
como el amanecer o el despertar.

(230)

In vain the words return
since they themselves still await
the hand that will break them and empty them
until they are unintelligible and pure
so that from them a different sense will be born
incomprehensible and clear
like dawn or waking.

In these lines the emphasis shifts momentarily from language to the language user, the strong poet who is able to remake language. The personified words themselves, however, put the poetic process in motion. The speaker presents himself as a "sonámbulo / entre las significaciones de la noche" [a sleepwalker / amid the meanings of night] (230). In the concluding lines of the poem he is relatively passive, obeying the mandate of language itself:

> hay algo que esas mismas palabras
> hastiadas de sí mismas, insistentes
> como una invitación o una súplica,
> nos obligan a hallar.
>
> (231)

> there is something that these very words
> disgusted with themselves, insistent
> like an invitation or a supplication
> oblige us to find.

Anita Hart, in a perceptive reading of this poem, concludes that "there is a tension between two factors: the urgency caused by 'the word' and experienced by the poet-speaker and the difficulty posed by the task of regenerating the capacity of language to offer creative expression."[8] It is language that drives the poetic speaker in his search for the truth. This is the case even though the words, invested with a humanlike will, are disgusted at their own inadequacy.

The poet, then, continues to believe in the potential power of language. A language that actually achieved this power, nevertheless, would be extremely rare if not impossible. Language in its degraded state is the rule, and poetry is the exception. Valente would probably subscribe to the view of Claudio Rodríguez, "Miserable el momento si no es canto ["Miserable the moment if it is not song"].[9] Only the moment of lyric transcendence, in other words, is exempt from the miserable norm. Valente expresses a similar sentiment at the beginning of another poem: "No puede a veces alzarse al canto lo que vive" ["At times what is alive cannot rise to the level of song"] (*Punto cero*, 232). This attitude is diametrically opposed to Jorge Guillén's belief that words as they are used every day easily acquire the power to represent a transcendent reality. For Guillén, transcendence is a daily event. Valente, characteristically, views the older poet's belief in everyday wonders as a paradox, identifying the poetic residue of *Cántico* with its darker moments (*Las palabras de la tribu*, 116).

As a consequence of the degraded state in which language is ordinarily found, Valente appears to denigrate words more frequently than he celebrates them. Yet the celebratory mode, though less common, occurs in certain "privileged moments":

> MOMENTOS privilegiados en los que sobre la escritura desciende en verdad la palabra y se hace cuerpo, materia de la encarnación. Incandescente torbellino inmóvil en la velocidad del centro y centro mismo de la quietud. (*Mandorla*, 49).

> Privileged moments when the word truly descends upon writing and becomes a body, matter of the incarnation. Incandescent whirlpool motionless in the velocity of the center and the very center of stillness.

This short prose poem illustrates logocentrism, the privileging of speech over writing, in a quite literal way. According to Derrida's familiar formulation, Western philosophy holds writing to be a less authentic form of language, since it can function in the absence of the speaker. Speech, in contrast, represents "the metaphysics of presence," the belief that the speaker's physical presence guarantees the meaning of his or her words.[10] The word *escritura* has several connotations here: it simultaneously evokes writing, *écriture* (in the Derridean sense), poetry, and sacred scripture. The written text, without the presence of the logos, is lifeless. In the extraordinary moments that the poet describes, the word *(palabra)* descends, from an implicitly superior position, in order to invest it with the living spirit of the truth. This word then takes its place as the still center in the middle of a whirlpool.

Valente explicitly equates the privileged moment of logocentrism with the doctrine of the incarnation: the word becomes flesh ("cuerpo, materia de la encarnación"). The doctrine of the resurrection of the flesh has captured the poet's imagination in a similar way, since it also implies a union between matter and spirit. Matter is no longer a lifeless substance, nor can spirit exist without its material dimension. With respect to language, linguistic form and linguistic meaning become inseparable as the body and soul of poetry. Valente has contended that the separation between the spiritual and the material is of Greek, not Christian origin. The doctrine of resurrection, which implies the reuniting of body and soul, must be distinguished from the mere belief in the immortality of the soul, which is common to many cultures. Included in *La piedra y el centro* [The stone and the center] a collection of essays on mysticism and poetic language, is an evocation of "El misterio del cuerpo cristiano" ["The mystery of the Christian body"]:

> Ciertas formas del pensamiento griego generan la escisión entre el alma y el cuerpo, que no es cristiana. Pues lo cristiano predica, en definitiva, la esencialidad, no la accidentalidad, de la carne y la unidad no tanto del alma o la psique como del espíritu o del pneuma con la materia. (*La piedra y el centro*, 24).

> Certain forms of Greek thought produce the division between soul and body, which is not Christian. For Christianity preaches, ultimately, the essential rather than accidental status of the flesh and the unity of matter with the spirit or *pneuma* more than with the soul or *psique*.

A major inspiration for this use of incarnation and resurrection as metaphors for poetic language is José Lezama Lima, the Cuban poet and theorist of poetry whom Valente has evoked in several poems and essays.[11] The doctrine of resurrection is one of the cornerstones of Lezama Lima's poetic system. In several essays, he opposes Heidegger's definition of the human being as a "ser para la muerte" [being for death] with the notion of a "ser para la resurrección" [being for resurrection]. Another kindred spirit is the Catalan artist Antoni Tàpies, who places a great emphasis on the materiality of his artistic medium.

Valente's belief in the material value of language places him in a tradition that does not recognize a significant difference between language and reality. In "Sobre la operación de las palabras sustanciales" ["Concerning the operation of substantial words"], another of the essays in *La piedra y el centro*, he explores various cultural and religious traditions that identify the materiality of the word with a sacred presence (*La piedra y el centro*, 51–59). Walter Ong, in a similar vein, has noted the close association between the oral word and the sense of sacredness: "The interiorizing force of the oral word relates in a special way to the sacral, to the ultimate concerns of existence. In most religions the spoken word functions integrally in ceremonial and devotional life."[12]

Ong goes on to describe the emphasis on orality in Christian theology:

> The spoken word is always an event, a movement in time, completely lacking in the thing-like repose of the written or printed word. In Trinitarian theology, the Second Person of the Godhead is the Word, and the human analogue for the Word is not the human written word but the human spoken word. God the Father "speaks" his Son; he does not inscribe him. . . . "The letter kills, the spirit [breath, on which rides the spoken word] gives life."[13]

Since Valente belongs to a literate rather than an oral culture, and is primarily a writer of texts rather than a public speaker, his logocentrism differs from that of the traditions he evokes in "Sobre la operación de las palabras sustanciales." His privileged moment occurs when the more authentically oral *palabra* rejoins the written text. The logocentric attempt to revivify writing with the magical presence of speech, of course, only makes sense within a context in which the written word has displaced the oral word. The poet undertakes to rescue the written text from its implicitly secondhand status.

In spite of his belief that poetic language should aim to be the dwelling place of the sacred, Valente is not a conventionally religious writer. His conception of the Word is logocentric, but, unlike that of Dante or San Juan de la Cruz, it is not theocentric. His interest in the religious function of poetic language, or in the parallels between mysticism and poetry, reflects a nostalgic attitude. This lack of religious faith produces a dilemma: the poet invests language with a sacred function, and yet the divine presence is perpetually deferred. The poet's task, paradoxically, is to prepare language to contain a sacred presence that never arrives. A second prose poem from *Mandorla* illustrates this idea:

> AGUARDÁBAMOS la palabra, y no llegó. No se dijo a sí misma. Estaba allí y aquí aún muda, grávida. Ahora no sabemos si la palabra es nosotros o éramos nosotros la palabra. Mas ni ella ni nosotros fuimos proferidos. Nada ni nadie en esta hora adviene, pues la soledad es la sola estancia del estar. Y nosotros aguardamos la palabra. (*Mandorla,* 44)

> We awaited the word, and it did not arrive. It did not pronounce itself. It was here or there still mute, pregnant. Now we do not know

> if the word is us or if we were the word. But neither it nor we were
> uttered. Nothing or nobody in this hour has an advent, for solitude
> is the only dwelling place of being. And we await the word.

The shift between the imperfect tense with which the poem begins and the present with which it ends implies that the arrival
of the word is indefinitely postponed. As in "Como una invitación
o una súplica," the word is personified and given the capacity for
autonomous action. It speaks itself rather than being spoken, and
its advent lies beyond the control of the group of people ("nosotros") who are awaiting it. The identification or confusion between language and its users adds a measure of ambiguity to this
situation, suggesting that the poetic word is not external to the
poet or to the reader. The reading or writing of poetry thus becomes a slow, contemplative, and introspective process of interpretation.

"Aguardábamos la palabra" suggests that the poet's metaphysics of presence is actually a metaphysics of the future. His
theory of the infinite signification of poetic language is an ideal
that his poems perpetually defer. For this reason, analyses that
demonstrate how Valente's poetry fulfills the conditions set forward in his theoretical statements overshoot the mark somewhat.
It is true that he makes similar statements in poems and essays:
his discursive works, whatever their ostensible subject, are almost
always a commentary on his own poetic aspirations. His poems,
however, cannot be considered practical applications of the theoretical guidelines proposed in his essays, since the poems are
themselves theoretical statements. In many cases, his self-conscious poetic manifestos refer not to their own practice but to an
ideally infinite language that is unrealizable by its very nature. In
the poetics of the ineffable, a poem that fails to live up to its stated
intention cannot necessarily be considered a failure, since its
aim—to say the unsayable—is never intended to be achievable.
This poetics, in other words, predicts a gap between theory
and practice.

The infinite deferral of presence tempers Valente's logocentric
impulses, permitting a more deconstructive interpretation of his
work. After an initial dissatisfaction with the state of everyday
language, the poet attempts to create a more authentic poetic
language. His newly sacralized language, in turn, is empty of

meaning, since the sacred *logos* never arrives to inhabit the text. This ultimate linguistic insufficiency must be distinguished from the earlier critique of degraded words. The problem is no longer the insufficiency of language to represent the sacred, but rather the absence of the sacred itself.

The poem that opens *Al dios del lugar* [To the god of the place], a book published in a series significantly entitled "Nuevos Textos Sagrados," presents a degraded version of the sacrament of communion:

> El vino tenía el vago color de la ceniza.
>
> Se bebía con un poso de sombra
> oscura, sombra, cuerpo
> mojado en las arenas.
>
> Llegaste aquí,
> viniste hasta esta noche.
>
> El insidioso fondo de la copa
> esconde a un dios incógnito.
>   Me diste
> a beber sangre
> en esta noche.
>   Fondo
> del dios bebido hasta las heces.
>
>   (*Al dios del lugar*, 13).

> The wine was the imprecise color of ash.
>
> It was drunk with its deposit of shadow,
> dark shadow, a wet body
> in the sands.
>
> You arrived here,
> you came to this night.
>
> The insidious bottom of the glass
> conceals an unknown god.
>   You gave me
> blood to drink
> on this night.
>   Bottom
> of the god drunk down to the dregs.

The speaker drinks a glass of ash-colored wine, brought to him, as is revealed toward the end of the poem, by an enigmatic night visitor. References to "cuerpo," "dios incógnito," and "sangre" situate this wine in the ritual context of the eucharist. The wine, transubstantiated into blood, is given negative associations. What makes the speaker willing to participate in this unpleasantly cannabilistic rite? The desire to reach a "deeper" level of reality is the motivating factor. The poem plays with the dual connotations of the idea of the depths ("el fondo"). Depth is *profundity* in the religious or philosophical sense of the term, and at the same time it is linked metaphorically to lowness and degradation. The bottom of the glass is called insidious, perhaps, because it suggests these two contradictory notions. The descent to a more profound level simultaneously brings the speaker down. To drink to the bottom of the cup is to reach the truth, but also to swallow the dregs. The word *insidioso* contains within itself *dios,* although the two words are not etymologically related. The manifestation of god as a word, at the literal level of the text, takes the form of a subtle deception. (By "literal" I refer to the actual letters of the text rather than to its nonmetaphorical level.)

The first poem of *Al dios del lugar,* then, is a sacred text mainly in a negative sense. It does portray a ritual act in which the speaker participates with great solemnity, but it simultaneously empties this act of value, deconstructing the illusory presence of the divine word. This frustrated act of communion with the *logos* points to a paradox in Valente's position: he is a religious poet without a religion. Putting his faith in the sacred power of the poetic word, he ultimately views the sacred itself as a self-subverting fiction. In spite of his insistence on the religious function of poetic language, he questions the truth-claims offered by religion.

The preceding analysis of Valente's ambivalent logocentrism can help to clarify his relation to earlier poets as well as to his contemporaries. Valente's view of poetic language is more dialectical than that of the poets studied in the first three chapters of this book. It would be an oversimplification to say that he has less faith in language than Guillén, Salinas, or Aleixandre, since he demands more of the poetic word than they do.[14] These older poets do not consider poetic language in a specifically sacred context, whether in a positive or negative sense. They are not logocentric, in the specific sense I have given the term in the chapter, but neither do they deconstruct logocentrism in the same way. Valente's divergence from Guillén's poetics is especially marked. The author of *Lenguaje y poesía* attempts to confine poetic language to the realm of the sayable, ruling the ineffable off limits. The younger poet's reversal of Guillén's position is symmetrical: Valente denies the value of a language that is adequate to the reality it purports to represent, identifying the poetic exclusively with the unsayable.

Valente's relation to Salinas and Aleixandre is not as clear-cut. In general terms, Valente invests poetic language more heavily with ethical and religious value. Salinas interprets the Mallarméan ideal of pure poetry in playful terms, whereas Valente undertakes the purification of poetic language as a moral imperative. Aleixandre, whose later poetry coincides chronologically with Valente's formative years, is close to his younger colleague in poetic terms as well. Both writers struggle with the problem of the ineffable, the expression of the inexpressible. Aleixandre, though, has less of a stake in an ideal poetic language: for him, language always remains opposed to the vitality of the extralinguistic reality that it mirrors. Comparisons between Valente and other precursor poets would also be relevant: for example, Luis Cernuda's personal and poetic example was extremely important for many younger poets of the 1950s and 1960s. No previous Spanish poet, however, anticipates Valente's conflicted creation and deconstruction of the poetic *logos*.

Among Valente's immediate contemporaries, Claudio Rodríguez offers the closest parallel, in spite of the apparent dissimilarity between Rodríguez's exuberant metaphorical richness and Valente's more austere manner. The kinship between the two poets occurs at the level of poetics rather than of style or tone. Rodríguez, like his generational companion, employs Christian concepts and images—especially grace, communion, and the eucharist—in an ambiguous way; he too borrows values from this religious tradition while questioning its ultimate validity. Both poets simultaneously exalt and denigrate language, investing it with a quasi-sacred power and questioning its ultimate validity. They also explore the paradoxical materiality and spirituality of the poetic sign. The dialectical view of language that dominates both poets' work produces a hermeneutical dilemma: the interpreter must decide whether to emphasize the poet's logocentric aspirations or the deconstruction of these aspirations.[15]

Many other poets who are commonly linked to Valente and Rodríguez do not give poetic language the same exalted status. This is not to say that they use language inexpertly, but simply that they do not invest it with the same overriding power and significance. Angel González and Gloria Fuertes, for example, are ingenious poets whose intertextual linguistic play does not give the *logos* a transcendent role. The divergence between Valente and a good number of his contemporaries calls into question some widespread critical assumptions about the unity of this group. Andrew Debicki's insights into the general tendencies shared by the poets of this "generation" have been accepted by many researchers in the field. In the 1990s the differences among the most prominent poets of this group are coming into sharper focus, as individual writers develop in different directions.

The later Valente's increased interest in the poetics of silence calls into question one of Debicki's most important premises: the notion of an apparently ordinary language.[16] One of Debicki's stated aims was to differentiate these poets from the realist poetics of the first generation of postwar Spanish poets, such as Blas de Otero, Angela Figuera, and Gabriel Celaya. His argument was that these poets were only *apparently* realist, that their use of subtle techniques to evoke reader-response allowed them to transcend the narrower limits of earlier postwar poetics. Analyzing several poems from Valente's first book, *A modo de esperanza* [By way of hope] (1955), Debicki finds that "In each of them Valente offers a clear and seemingly 'realistic' vision or narrative, which in itself holds meaning. . . . Yet each of them also leads us, on subsequent readings, to perceive new dimensions created by hitherto unsuspected codes and patterns."[17]

From a later vantage point, the originality of the younger poets of the 1950s is more obvious to both readers and critics, in part because of the way in which they have developed in more recent years. In hindsight, Debicki's assertion that the apogee of these poets was the fifteen-year period from 1956 until 1971 is open to debate.[18] While Jaime Gil de Biedma remained silent during the last decades of his life, Valente, Rodríguez, González, Gamoneda, and Brines are the authors of a good part of the most important poetry published during the period between 1970 and 1990. Reading the later work of some of these poets, it is difficult to understand the earlier critical tendency to view them as part of a postwar realist tradition. This initial assumption, however, came naturally to readers in the 1950s and 1960s, when many of these poets had not yet clearly renounced the postulates of social poetry.

The notion of a deceptively realist style becomes much less relevant for the interpretation of Valente's mature work; rereading remains an important part of the process, of course, but the initial reading no longer yields a "seemingly realistic" vision. The later Valente's insistence on the separation between poetic language and ordinary language is absolute: "Sin una consideración de esa palabra total, toda consideración en profundidad de lo poético está negada de antemano. En efecto, lo poético exige como requisito primero el descondicionamiento del lenguaje como instrumentalidad. El lenguaje concebido como sola instrumentalidad deja de participar en la palabra" ["Without a consideration of this total word, any profound consideration of the poetic is doomed from the outset. In effect, the poetic demands as its first requirement the deconditioning of language as instrumentality. Language conceived of as mere instrumentality no longer forms part of the word"] (La piedra y el centro, 52). The disruption of utilitarian language, then, is the first step in the creation of an authentically poetic Word. The conception of language found in Valente's poetry since the later 1970s takes him far from the dominant realist assumptions of the postwar period.

The two chapters that follow this one will explore the work of two other prominent poets of Valente's age-group. Antonio Gamoneda's Descripción de la mentira, a little-studied work by an excellent though relatively unknown poet, explores the contradictions inherent in an exalted poetic rhetoric that renounces its grounding in the truth. Gamoneda's poetic position is quite similar to that of both Valente and Rodríguez. An equally significant poet, Jaime Gil de Biedma, departs considerably from the Valente's poetics of the sacred. A reading of his work will thus further question the premise that the poets of this cohort share a common approach to poetic language.

5

Rhetoric and Truth in Antonio Gamoneda's *Descripción de la mentira*

Antonio Gamoneda is absent from the major anthologies and critical studies of the poetry of the Generation of the 1950s, the group to which he belongs chronologically. Born in Oviedo in 1931, Gamoneda is a contemporary of better-known poets such as Claudio Rodríguez, José Angel Valente, and Jaime Gil de Biedma. Due largely to extrapoetic circumstances, however, he neither established close ties with other poets of his age-group nor gained early fame as a poet. Living in geographical isolation in León, Gamoneda did not begin to publish his most significant poetry until the late 1970s. Existing criticism of his work treats him in a regional rather than a national context.[1]

Gamoneda's first published book, *Sublevación inmóvil* [Immobile rebellion], was runner-up for the prestigious Adonais prize in 1960, the year in which Francisco Brines won for *Las brasas*. Gamoneda did not publish another book until 1977, the year in which *Descripción de la mentira* [Description of the lie] appeared in print. This book, a single long poem divided into several sections, is Gamoneda's single most significant work and the one that finally established his place in contemporary Spanish poetry. The case of *Blues castellano* [Castilian Blues], written between 1961 and 1966, is typical of Gamoneda's marginality within his generational group. Had this volume been published in a timely fashion, it could have coincided with the poetic apogee of the group: many of the most significant books of his contemporaries, including Brines's *Palabras a la oscuridad*, Valente's *La memoria y los signos*, Rodríguez's *Alianza y condena*, and Gil de Biedma's *Moralidades*, were published in the midsixties, whereas Gamoneda's book did not see the light of day until 1982.

Despite Gamoneda's geographical and historical marginality, his work is in many ways typical of the poetry written by his contemporaries. Friendship among poets does not produce stylistic uniformity, nor does geographical isolation necessarily lead to eccentricity. Gamoneda's voice is a unique one, but this is equally true of the other major poets of the period. Like other poets who began to write during the 1950s, his early work reflects a concern with the problems raised by the social and existential poets of the 1940s and 1950s. León was an important center of social poetry. According to Miguel Casado, Gamoneda "Desde el 'exterior,' mantuvo una cierta relación con los grupos de *Espadaña y Claraboya*" ["From 'outside' maintained a certain relationship with the *Espadaña* and *Claraboya* groups"]—two important journals of socially committed poetry.[2] Blas de Otero's *Angel fieramente humano* is a major influence on some of the sonnets included in Gamoneda's *La tierra y los labios* [Earth and lips] (1947–1953):

> ¡Cuánta luz, cuánto hielo, cuánta nada!
> Ahora, donde Dios era de fuego,
> donde hablaba el dolor, llora el vacío.
>
> (*Edad*, 95)

> What light, what ice, what nothingness!
> Now, in the place where God was fire,
> where sorrow spoke, the void weeps.

Blues castellano includes poems that link the poet's personal experience to larger social concerns:

> Va a hacer diecinueve años
> que trabajo para un amo.
> Hace diecinueve años que me da la comida
> y todavía no he visto su rostro.
>
> No he visto al amo en diecinueve años
> pero todos los días yo me miro a mí mismo
> y ya voy sabiendo poco a poco
> cómo es el rostro del amo.
>
> (*Edad*, 180)

> It will be nineteen years now
> since I began to work for the boss.

> For nineteen years he's been feeding me,
> and I still have not seen his face.
>
> I haven't seen the boss in nineteen years,
> but every day I look at myself,
> and now I'm beginning to discover, little by little,
> what the boss' face is like.

As these opening stanzas of "Blues del amo" illustrate, Gamoneda's perspective differs from that of many other socially committed poets in that he speaks as a member of the working class rather than as a middle-class sympathizer.

Descripción de la mentira (1977) exemplifies the metapoetry practiced by Spanish poets during the 1960s and 1970s. Although Gamoneda's poetic style is highly individual, the position that he takes in this book is quite close to that of José Angel Valente and Claudio Rodríguez. Like these poets, Gamoneda interrogates the inherent ambiguity of language in ethical terms. The title of the book implies a concern with truth and falsity. Rather than searching for the truth directly, however, the poet forges a self-consciously duplicitous poetic dialect that denounces its own falseness.

Since the major theme of *Descripción de la mentira* is language, the characteristic style that Gamoneda develops in the poem reinforces the overall intention that he envisions for his poetic act. A device frequently used in the poem is the self-consuming paradox, the statement that destroys the very ground upon which it affirms its truth claims: "Yo en tu lugar mentiría más dulcemente" [If I were you I would lie more sweetly] (*Edad,* 247). This key sentence, repeated several times in the poem, remains open to multiple interpretations. It could be read ironically, if we presume that the speaker stands on the side of truth. Taken literally, the statement subverts its own reliability, since it recommends a less abrasive form of deceit. A concern with the difficulty of finding the truth is one that Gamoneda shares with both José Angel Valente and Claudio Rodríguez. In "Brujas a mediodía," from *Alianza y Condena*, Rodríguez poses the conflict between truth and human desire as an aporia:

> ¿Por qué quien ama nunca
> busca verdad, sino que busca dicha?

¿Cómo sin la verdad
puede existir la dicha? He aquí todo.[3]

Why does the lover never
seek truth, but only happiness?
How without truth
can happiness exist? This is everything.

In both Rodríguez and Gamoneda, truth enters into a conflict with the human desire for happiness in such a way that neither alternative is wholly satisfactory. Gamoneda perhaps goes even further than Rodríguez in questioning the viability of an absolute truth.

Another major feature of Gamoneda's style is the combination of a solemn, portentous tone with highly concrete references to specific objects. The impression produced through this technique is that of a highly detailed but ultimately undecipherable symbolic code:

Las hortensias extendidas en otro tiempo decoran la estancia más
   arriba de mi cuerpo.

He sentido el grito de los faisanes acorralados en las ramas de
   agosto.

(*Edad*, 257)

The hydrangeas extended in another time decorate the room
   above my body.
I have heard the cry of the pheasants corralled in the branches of
   August.

The specificity of the references—"hortensias" and "faisanes" rather than generic flowers and birds—suggests but does not deliver a precise symbolic import. The poetic voice withholds the information that the reader would require in order to interpret these object metaphorically or, alternatively, to situate them in a more literal context.

Few important Spanish poets of the twentieth century have experimented with extended poetic forms. Much more frequent are the highly unified sequences of lyric poems produced by Juan Ramón Jiménez (*Diario de un poeta recién casado, Dios deseado o deseante),* Salinas *(La voz a ti debida),* or Claudio Rodríguez *(Don de la ebriedad),* to name only some of the better-known examples. A long poem like *Descripción de una mentira* is an apparent exception to this tendency. Miguel Casado, whose excellent introduction to Gamoneda's collected poetry is one of the few scholarly studies of the poet to date, calls attention to the narrative aspect of the book. *Descripción de la mentira,* however, is an extended lyric meditation, not an epic poem. As Casado notes, the beginning and end points are identical: "Parecen, pues, coincidir el inicio y el fin del recorrido" ["The beginning and the end of the journey, then, seem to coincide"] *(Edad,* 30). Individual events are narrated in the past tense throughout the poem, but these events only occasionally cohere as a narrative sequence.

One way in which Gamoneda disrupts narrative continuity is through his verse form. The basic unit of versification in the poem is a fairly long, self-contained *versículo,* a line that is not quite long enough to form a paragraph of prose. The lines are separated typographically by fairly large blank spaces. Longer pauses, indicated by larger spaces, separate clusters of *versículos,* while the poem as a whole is divided into twenty-two unnumbered sections, marked only by page breaks. The overall effect of these divisions is to focus attention on the individual line and thus to slow the pace of reading.

It would be difficult to summarize the "plot" of *Descripción de la mentira,* since its coherence is thematic rather than narrative. The problem for the critic is that the length of the poem (some fifty pages in Casado's edition) makes the conventional method of line-by-line textual analysis awkward and impractical. The alternative I have chosen to an exhaustive reading of the text in its entirety is a close examination of the first, five-page, section of the poem. The principal achievement of Gamoneda's work is the creation of an individual poetic language. Although *Descripción de la mentira* contains other explicitly metapoetic passages, the first section serves as a prologue in which the poet states his intentions, establishes his status as a speaker, and lays out the essential parameters of his discourse. Although an equally detailed reading of the other sections of the poem would produce additional observations, such an attempt at completeness would be subject to the law of diminishing returns, especially since Gamoneda's poetic discourse is highly reiterative.

Descripción de la mentira opens with a brief narration in the past tense of the circumstances that led up to the actual writing of the poem:

El óxido se posó en mi lengua como el sabor de una
    desaparición.

El olvido entró en mi lengua y no tuve otra conducta que el
    olvido,

y no acepté otro valor que la imposibilidad.

Como un barco calcificado en un país del que se ha retirado el
    mar,

escuché la rendición de mis huesos depositándose en el
    descanso;

escuché la huida de los insectos y la retracción de la sombra al
    ingresar en lo que quedaba de mí;

escuché hasta que la verdad dejó de existir en el espacio y en mi
    espíritu,

y no pude resistir la perfección del silencio.

(*Edad*, 235)

Rust settled on my tongue like the taste of a disappearance. / Oblivion entered my tongue and I had no conduct other than oblivion, / and I accepted no courage other than impossibility. / Like a calcified ship in a country from which the sea has withdrawn, / I listened to my bones surrender as they settled down in rest; / I listened to the insects escape and the shadow shrinking as I entered into what remained of me; / I listened until truth ceased to exist in space and in my spirit, / and I could not resist the temptation of silence.

In this passage the speaker presents himself as a passive recipient, or even a victim, of forces beyond his control that impose silence upon him. His inability to speak is presented as his only possible alternative; he can only listen to the events that are happening to him, including the process of his own aging. The comparison between the speaker and the calcified ship suggests that the transcendent role of the poet had lost both its viability and its grounding in the truth.

Just as his previous silence was imposed rather than chosen, the speaker's present words do not result from an act of will, but from an inexorable obligation. He does not elect to speak as a poet. Rather, it is the poetic act that chooses him. The second passage begins: "No creo en las invocaciones pero las invocaciones creen en mí: / han venido otra vez como líquenes inevitables" ["I do not believe in invocations but invocations believe in me: / they have come once again like inevitable lichens"] (*Edad*, 235)[4] The inevitability and necessity of writing is linked to the almost supernatural power of the poetic voice, described in the third and fourth passages:

> Ahora es verano y me proveo de alquitranes y espinas y lápices iniciados.
>
> y las sentencias suben hacia las cánulas de mis oídos.
>
>
> He salido de la habitación obstinada.
>
> Puedo hallar leche en frutos abandonados y escuchar llanto en un hospital vacío.
>
> La prosperidad de mi lengua se revela en cuanto fue olvidado durante mucho tiempo y sin embargo visitado por las aguas.
>
> (*Edad*, 236)

> Now it is summer and I furnish myself with tar and thorns and initiated pencils, / and the proverbs rise to my ear canals. / / I have left the obstinate room. / I can find milk in abandoned fruit and listen to weeping in an empty hospital. / My tongue's prosperity shows in everything forgotten for a long time and nevertheless visited by the waters.

The speaker, furnished with magical pencils and other tools of his trade, is invaded by a prophetic discourse. He claims access to a special mode of perception, a privileged insight through which he is able to discern both positive and negative forces, the hidden potential of nature and the residual human sorrow lingering in empty hospitals. In contrast to the self-deprecation implicit in the image of the calcified ship, the speaker now boasts of the capacity of his poetic speech to revitalize forgotten realities.

This passage continues with a description of the period of silence that preceded the composition of the poem we are reading:

> Este es un año de cansancio. Verdaderamente es un año muy
>   viejo.
>
> Este es el año de la necesidad.
>
> Durante quinientas semanas he estado ausente de mis designios,
>
> depositado en nódulos y silencioso hasta la maldición.
>
> Mientras tanto la tortura ha pactado con las palabras.
>   (*Edad*, 236–37)

> This is a year of tiredness. Truly it is a very old year. / This is the year of necessity. / For five hundred weeks I have been absent from my designs, / deposited in nodules and silent to the point of cursing. / Meanwhile torture has made a pact with words.

The speaker emphasizes the necessity of beginning to write again after a long poetic silence that roughly corresponds, in Gamoneda's career, to the first half of the 1970s, following the steadier poetic production of the previous decade. The poems of *Blues castellano* belong to the first half of the 1960s, while *Pasión de la mirada* [Passion of the gaze], written between 1963 and 1970, contains only twenty-four poems. Gamoneda's public silence was even more pronounced, since these works were not published until much later. It is implied that the poet's inability to perform his appointed tasks during this period has somehow permitted an alliance between language and torture to develop.

The solemn tone of these lines, seen in the quasi-biblical expression "quinientas semanas" and the rather pretentious "designios," emphasizes the great importance attributed to the act of poetic speech, which is clearly an ethical imperative in the "año de la necesidad." Yet the speaker's lack of autonomous will makes his return to poetry at this particular moment seem arbitrary. For entirely unexplained reasons, a face begins to smile at him and grants him once again a state of grace:

> Ahora un rostro sonríe y su sonrisa se deposita sobre mis labios.
>
> y la advertencia de su música explica todas las pérdidas y me acompaña.
>
> Habla de mí como una vibración de pájaros que hubiesen desaparecido y retornasen;
>
> habla de mí con labios que todavía responden a la dulzura de unos párpados.
>
> (*Edad*, 237)

Now a face smiles and its smile settles on my lips / and the warning in its music explains all losses and accompanies me. / It speaks of me like a vibration of words that have disappeared and are now returning; / it speaks to me with lips that still respond to the sweetness of someone's eyelids.

In the fifth, and longest, passage in the first section, the speaker switches to the future tense in order to state his intentions:

> En este país, en este tiempo cuya pesadumbre se dibuja en lápidas de mercurio,
>
> voy a extender mis brazos y penetrar la hierba,
>
> voy a deslizarme en la espesura del acebo para que tú me adviertas, para que me convoques en la humedad de tus axilas.
>
> Todavía existe luz en la destitución y mi valor se descubre en sílabas en las que tú y los rostros actuáis como gránulos silvestres,
>
> como espermas excitadas hasta penetrar en la bujía del sonido,
>
> hasta sumergir mi cuerpo en aguas que no palpitan,
>
> hasta cubrir mi rostro con las pomadas de la majestad.
>
> (*Edad*, 237)

In this country, in this time whose affliction is outlined on tablets of mercury, / I will stretch out my arms and penetrate the grass, / I will slide into the thick holly branches so that you can warn me, so that you can summon me with the dampness of your armpits. / Destitution still contains light and my courage emerges in syllables in which you and the faces behave like wild granules, / like sperm excited until they penetrate the candle of sound, / until they submerge my body in waters that do not throb, / until they cover my face with majestic ointments.

The exalted tone of these lines reinforces the privileged status of the poetic speaker, who transforms himself rhetorically from a concrete historical individual into a transcendent force. In this way the power of the poetic voice is detached from the poet's concrete biographical identity. The speaker must respond to a contradictory imperative: to speak in convincing tones, with a prophetic voice, but not to arrogate to himself any excessive power or privilege. His responsibility and power as a poet are great, yet do not belong to him as an individual.

The precursors of Gamoneda's poetic voice are the social poets of the postwar period, such as Blas de Otero, who manifested their solidarity with the oppressed working class. It is interesting to note that despite Gamoneda's proletarian origins, he does not escape from the double-bind inherent in the expression of this solidarity. The social poet attempts to merge his voice with that of the common people. The assumption of a prophetic voice, however, always implies some degree of distance between the *pueblo* and its spokesperson.

This passage continues with an attempt to resolve the contradiction between this important role and the humility required of the spokesperson for a humble reality that includes both human beings and nature itself. After mentioning "las pomadas de la majestad," the speaker quickly rectifies himself in order to reject the implication that he belongs to royalty:

No es una glorificación, no es que la púrpura haya caído sobre
  mis huesos;

es más hermoso y antiguo: alentar sobre el vinagre hasta volverlo
  azul, adelantar un cuchillo y retirarlo húmedo de una
  exudación que dignifica al esgrimidor.

Agradezco la pobreza para que la pobreza no me maldiga y me
  conceda anillos que me distingan de cuando fui puro y
  legislaba en la negación.

Huelo los testimonios de cuanto es sucio sobre la tierra y no me
reconcilio pero amo lo que ha quedado de nosotros.

Estoy viejo de mí mismo pero hay estigmas. Han llegado los
visitantes. Hay hormigas debajo de las llagas.

Siento la fertilidad que se refugia entre la ira de mis cabellos y
oigo el deslizamiento de las especies que nos han abandonado.

He cesado en la compasión porque la compasión me entregaba a
príncipes funestos cuyas medallas se hundían en el corazón de
mis hijas.

                                                                (*Edad*, 238)

It is not a glorification, it's not that purple has fallen upon my bones; /
it's more beautiful and ancient: breathing on vinegar until it turns
blue, thrusting out a knife and pulling it back moist from an exudation
that dignifies the fencer. / I am grateful to poverty so that poverty
will not curse me and will give me rings to distinguish me from
when I was pure and legislated in denial. / I smell the testimonies of
everything on earth that is dirty and I don't reconcile myself to it but
I love what remains of us. / I'm old to myself but there are stigmas.
The visitors have arrived. Ants crawl beneath wounds. / I feel the
fertility that takes refuge in the anger of my hair and I hear the species
that have abandoned us slide away. / I've given up compassion because compassion surrendered me to baneful princes whose medals
sank into my daughters' hearts.

These lines, some of the more difficult in the poem, reflect the
influence of prewar surrealist poets such as Lorca and Aleixandre.
What is clear is that the poet enters into symbolic combat against
the "príncipes," presumably the privileged rulers of his country.
His stature derives from the nobility of this struggle ("una exudación que dignifica el esgrimidor"), but his primary identification
is with the oppressed and suffering, including his own daughters.
    In spite of the speaker's clear expression of solidarity, there are
paradoxical elements in his rhetoric. One would expect him to
feel compassion for the victims of the "príncipes," for example,
but he explicitly rejects this sentiment. Gamoneda's use of such
paradoxes sets him apart from the self-confident rhetoric of the
social poets, whose poetic goals he shares to a large extent. While
the social poets would never call into question the truthfulness
of their own discourse, this is exactly the speaker's strategy in the

final lines of this passage. The truth, which had abandoned him during his long poetic dry spell, will not serve as a weapon against the oppressor, nor as a means of validating his poetic voice:

> Yo haré con los príncipes una destilación que será nociva para
> ellos pero excitante y dulce en la población como lo es el zumo
> reservado en vasijas muy oscuras.
>
> No recurriré a la verdad porque la verdad ha dicho no y ha
> puesto ácidos en mi cuerpo y me ha separado de la exaltación.
>
> ¿Qué verdad existe en el vientre de las palomas?
>
> ¿La verdad está en la lengua o en el espacio de los espejos?
>
> ¿La verdad es lo que responde a las preguntas de los príncipes?
>
> ¿Cuál es entonces la respuesta a las preguntas de los alfareros?
> (*Edad*, 238–39)

I will make a distillation from the princes that will be poisonous to them but exciting and sweet to the populace, like a juice reserved in the darkest vessels. / I will not have recourse to the truth because the truth has said no and has put acid in my body and has separated me from exaltation. / What truth exists in the belly of doves? / Does truth dwell in the tongue or in the space of mirrors? / Is the truth what answers the princes' questions? / What, then, is the answer to the questions of the potters?

The questions posed in this passage are of a special variety. They are not rhetorical questions with self-evident answers, questions that could be replaced by simple statements. Instead, they belong to the class of rhetorical questions that simply cannot be answered at all, since the information they request presumably transcends human knowledge altogether. The speaker's questions dramatize a fundamental lack of epistemological foundation: it is impossible to decide where the truth resides. The impossibility of responding to these questions is heightened through the use of private symbolism: "el vientre de las palomas," "las preguntas de los alfareros." Nevertheless, the questions are meaningful and their answers do matter. For example, "¿La verdad está en la lengua o en el espacio de los espejos?," is an attempt to locate the truth. Does it reside in language itself, in the speaker's physical tongue ("la lengua" in its more literal meaning), or in an unreal world of mirror images? The question is ambiguous in that the conjunction *o* can be read in two contradictory ways, either as opposing the two alternatives or linking them together. In equally meaningful fashion, the penultimate line—"La verdad es lo que responde a las preguntas de los príncipes"—poses the poet's dilemma in very clear terms: Is the truth an adequate response to the power represented by the princes?

The following passage begins by contrasting the question with a more concrete physical reality, the body, but then continues with a further series of rhetorical questions:

> Si levantas una túnica encontrarás un cuerpo pero no una
>   pregunta:
>
> ¿para qué las palabras desecadas en cíngulos o las construidas en
>   esquinas inmóviles,
>
> las instruidas en láminas y, luego, desposeídas y ávidas?
>
> Y bien: ¿he sido yo alguna vez cínico como asfalto o pelambre?
>
> No es así sino que el asfalto poseía mi memoria y mis
>   exclamaciones relataban la perdición y la enemistad.
>
> Nuestra dicha es difícil recluida en la belladona y en recipientes
>   que no deben ser abiertos.
>
> Sucio, sucio es el mundo; pero respira. Y tú entras en la
>   habitación como un animal resplandeciente.
>
> (*Edad*, 239)

If you raise a tunic you will find a body but not a question: / what use are words that have been dried in cingula or constructed in motionless corners / those instructed in engravings and then dispossessed and greedy? / Fine: but have I too been cynical like asphalt or knotted hair? / That's not it: the asphalt possessed my memory and my exclamations told of perdition and enmity. / / Our joy is difficult, enclosed in belladonna and in receptacles that shouldn't be opened. / Filthy, filthy is the world; but it breathes. And you enter the room like a radiant animal.

The reality of the physical body contrasts with the unanswerable rhetorical questions in the previous passage. The speaker continues to pose such questions, however, in order to question the efficacy of poetic language—"¿para qué las palabras . . . ?"—and to examine his own conscience. He refers again to the state of silence that precedes the writing of the poem. By rejecting the idea that he has been guilty of cynicism, he once again shifts attention away from the idea of moral agency in order to emphasize his status as a victim of inexorable forces ("el asfalto poseía mi memoria"). During this dark period, it was not the poet himself, but his "exclamaciones" that expressed his destructive sentiments.

The eighth and final passage of this section of *Descripción de la mentira* resumes with a final rhetorical question:

Después del conocimiento y el olvido ¿qué pasión me concierne?

No he de responder sino reunirme con cuanto está ofrecido en
    los atrios y en la distribución de los residuos,

con cuanto tiembla y es amarillo debajo de la noche.
(Edad, 239)

After knowledge and oblivion, what passion concerns me? / I must not respond, but join everything offered in the courtyards and in the distribution of residues, / with everything that trembles and is yellow beneath the night.

At this point the speaker no longer attempts to respond to his own unanswerable questions, offering instead a less complicated gesture of solidarity, a gesture made possible through the quasi-magical powers attributed to the poetic voice. The writing of poetry is not so much an intellectual act, an attempt to understand the nature of the truth, as an attitude of passive and humble acceptance of the dirtiness of the world. The construction introduced by *cuanto*, repeated twice at the end of the section, conveys an indiscriminate openness to reality in all of its contradictory aspects.

The principal task accomplished in the first section of *Descripción de la mentira* is the legitimation of the speaker's poetic voice. To summarize briefly:

1. The poet's right to speak does not derive from his poetic talent or personal will; it is an inexorable semidivine calling.
2. His authority is immanent to his role as a poetic speaker, without pertaining to him as a person. During the period of his poetic muteness, his memory resembled asphalt.
3. His legitimacy as a poet and the power of his rhetoric stem from a feeling of solidarity with a vaguely defined subterranean world that includes both natural and human suffering.
4. Most importantly, the speaker specifically rejects the truth as a source of legitimacy. Language has become so inherently corrupt that the only alternative for the honest poet, paradoxically, is to undertake a "description of the lie," of a language that no longer claims to be grounded in transcendent truth.

The contemporary philosopher Richard Rorty has questioned the need for foundations for political and ethical positions. For Rorty, the validity of social values is pragmatically situated in a dialogic situation, but cannot be established in rigorously philosophical terms. Gamoneda's attempt to justify the act of poetic speech is equally pragmatic. By discounting truth as his means of legitimation, he obliges the reader to accept (or reject) his rhetoric as a self-consciously fictive discourse. Gamoneda might qualify as one of Rorty's "liberal ironists," who are able to combine "commitment with a sense of the contingency of their own commitment."[5] Not coincidentally, Rorty attributes an appreciation of this contingency to poets rather than to philosophers.[6] It is important to note that Rorty continues to believe that social solidarity is desirable: he simply rejects the necessity of philosophical justifications of this solidarity.

In light of this reading of *Descripción de la mentira,* a rethinking of the relation of Gamoneda to his generational counterparts is in order. The similarity between Gamoneda and poets such as Valente, Rodríguez, and Gil de Biedma does not occur at the level of style. Carlos Barral, another poet of this age-group, has noted that there is no single group style: "Yo diría que es un grupo poco o nada unitario, en el que las semejanzas se pueden encadenar de dos en dos poetas, lo que hace—por ejemplo—que yo me parezca algo a Jaime Gil de Biedma, que Gil de Biedma se parezca algo a José Angel Valente y que éste se parezca menos a mí" [I would say that it is a group that is not unified very much or at all, in which the similarities might link poets in pairs, so that, for example, I resemble Jaime Gil de Biedma somewhat, Gil de Biedma resembles José Angel Valente, and that Valente is less similar to me"].[7] Gamoneda does not closely resemble any other single poet of this group, and thus would not form a part of this chain. He does, however, confront a similar set of problems involving the social and ethical function of poetic language. Like many of his generational counterparts, he combines a postmodern lack of faith in epistemological certainly with a commitment to the poet's social role. Like his contemporaries, he questions the capacity of poetic language to contain the truth, but he continues to emphasize the important function of the poet as spokesperson for the oppressed.

Jaime Gil de Biedma, the subject of the next chapter, takes this pragmatic view of the poet's function one step further. Unlike Valente and Gamoneda, he does not adopt the rhetoric of poetic prophecy. In Gil de Biedma's work, poetic language is no longer the dwelling place of the sacred or the inexorable voice of an oppressed reality. It becomes, instead, a medium for evaluating the ethical problems of human experience in a lucidly self-conscious way.

6

Jaime Gil de Biedma's *Moralidades:*
Rationalism and Poetic Form

Several important contemporary Spanish poets view the creative process as a means of uncovering a previously unknown experience; they thus emphasize the irrational, intuitive, and unpredictable character of poetic composition. José Angel Valente's definition of poetry as "un conocimiento 'haciéndose'" ["knowledge in the process of formation"] is a succinct and frequently quoted formulation of this generational topos.[1] Jaime Gil de Biedma, as I shall argue in this chapter, proposes a rationalist model of poetic creation, one that is substantially different from that shared by José Angel Valente, Claudio Rodríguez, and other poets who published their first books in the decade of the 1950s.[2] One critic, Juan José Lanz, has claimed that Gil de Biedma's work is fundamentally irrationalist.[3] Without disputing the evidence Lanz adduces, I would distinguish between the poet's occasional use of irrational metaphors, along with similar techniques that are the common heritage of modern literature, from his overall attitude toward the creative act. I would also dispute Lanz's characterization of the "irrealismo" of Gil de Biedma's poetry, since more often than not the poet's aim is to criticize and unmask irreality rather than to perpetuate it.

Gil de Biedma explicitly questions the organicist identification between form and content that underlies the poetics of other important poets of the Generation of the 1950s, including Rodríguez, Gamoneda, and Valente. This rejection does not entail a simple return to a poetics of communication, in which the poet transmits a previously known message to the reader. In Gil de Biedma's work, rather, poetic form becomes a means of controlling and modifying the poet's initial experience. Form is no longer organically linked to content. Rather, the autonomy of form serves as a sign of the poet's self-mastery. In an essay on Baudelaire, Gil de Biedma compares his own reaction to the French poet's work to that of Claudio Rodríguez: "Recuerdo haber oído hablar a un poeta muy joven admirador de Rimbaud, de la excesiva coherencia lógica y formal de Baudelaire y del despliegue en exceso previsible de sus poemas" ["I remember hearing a young poet, a great admirer of Rimbaud, speak of Baudelaire's excessive logical and formal coherence and of the excessively predictable development of his poems"].[4] Gil de Biedma argues that Baudelaire's more lucid approach to writing is capable of producing more surprising results than the spontaneous irrationalism of Rimbaud and his French surrealist heirs.[5] This contrast between Rimbaud and Baudelaire illuminates the difference between Rodríguez, an "inspired" Rimbaldian poet (especially in his early work), and the more lucid attitude of Gil de Biedma himself. Gil de Biedma is known as an extremely slow and painstaking writer, a perfectionist who wrote very few poems in the final two decades of his life. While Rodríguez has also published very little in recent years, this is perhaps the result of his dependence on a fundamentally irrational poetic inspiration.

Like his master Luis Cernuda, Gil de Biedma is heavily steeped in the Anglo-American poetic tradition. He translates W. H. Auden and imitates Byron's comic style—in rather awkward English verse.[6] He is especially indebted to British modernism: his introduction to his translation of T. S. Eliot's *The Uses of Poetry and the Uses of Criticism* includes an incisive statement on the "generational" polemic concerning *comunicación* and *conocimiento*.[7] A telling fact about Gil de Biedma's interest in English-language literature is that he tends to favor its more aesthetically conservative tendencies: Eliot and Auden rather than William Carlos Williams or Gertrude Stein. I do not mean to imply that Gil de Biedma is politically conservative; there is no necessary relation between his literary position and his political stance. In a statement for the back cover of *Las personas del verbo* Gil de Biedma defines his own politics in ambiguous terms: "He sido de izquierdas y es probable que siga siéndolo, pero hace tiempo que no ejerzo" ["I have been a leftist and I probably still am one, but I haven't been active for a while"]. The point is that he often aligns himself with the least experimental poets of Anglo-American modernism.

An especially revealing example of Gil de Biedma's conservative affinities is found in an epigraph to his 1966 *Moralidades* [Moralities]:

> The artistic process is one of moral evaluation of human experience, by means of a technique which renders possible an evaluation more precise than any other. The poet tries to understand his experience in rational terms, to state his understanding, and simultaneously to state, by means of the feelings which we attach to words, the kind and degree of emotion that should properly be motivated by this understanding.
>
> (Quoted in *Las personas del verbo*, 76)

These words are taken from *In Defense of Reason,* a critical study by the modern American poet Yvor Winters.[8] The salient aspects of Winters's poetic and critical work is its extreme rejection of the experimental tradition of modernist poetry. Although he began his career in the early 1920s as an imitator of Williams's free verse, Winters soon opted for fixed metrical form. His use of meter became an ethical imperative: poetic form, according to Winters, is the means by which the poet controls and evaluates emotion and experience. Winters even claimed to be able to judge a poem's ethical value, and by extension its aesthetic worth as well, by an examination of the relation of its metrical form to its emotional content. This is the theory summarized in the passage that Gil de Biedma chooses as his epigraph.

In Defense of Reason contains an earlier study, *Primitivism and Decadence* (1937), a moralistic condemnation of the irrationalism of modernist poetry. Read in its historical context, Winters's theory of poetic form is a decidedly antimodern statement. Of course, Gil de Biedma's appropriation of Winters's words does not mean that he subscribes to the American critic's views. Gil de Biedma, whose aesthetic stance is much closer to that of Eliot or Auden, would undoubtedly reject Winters's reactionary Christianity as well as the dogmatic way in which he expounds his views. Still, the epigraph does provide a convenient point of departure for the study of the poems collected in *Moralidades*. A central problem for Gil de Biedma, as for Valente, is the reconciliation of aesthetics and political commitment. The younger poets of the

1950s attempt to heal the rift between "social poetry" and the aesthetic innovations of modern poetry. Their solution to this problem is to develop a theory of sociopolitical commitment that focuses on poetic language rather than on theme alone. José Angel Valente's "punto cero" evokes Barthes's early investigation of the ethical value of literary form.[9] In similar fashion, Gil de Biedma strategically resurrects Winters's moralistic theory of form in order to emphasize the poet's conscious control over the communication of his experience.

The paragraph cited by Gil de Biedma continues as follows:

> The artistic result differs from the crude experience mainly in its refinement of judgment: the difference in really good art is enormous, but the difference is of degree rather than of kind. The intensity of the work of art, which is different from the intensity of the crude expression, lies in this: that what we call intensity in a work of art is a combination of the importance of the original subject and the precision of the judgment.[10]

This passage is an attempt to refute T. S. Eliot's contention that the poet should be an impersonal catalyst in the creation of poetry rather than an active agent. For Winters, Eliot's avowed passivity is tantamount to a refusal to assume a consciously ethical stance. Gil de Biedma's "poetry of experience"[11] is similar in conception to Winters's notion that the poet's main artistic task is to evaluate his or her previous experience in explicitly ethical terms. This is precisely the procedure followed in such poems as "Intento formular mis experiencias de la guerra" ["I attempt to formulate my experiences of the war"] and "Barcelona ja no es bona" ["Barcelona is no longer good"] (*Las personas del verbo*, 122–24; 79–81), which are retrospective critiques of the poet's naive childhood view of the war and of his parents' prewar bourgeois lifestyle.

Winters's striking notion that form is the litmus test of the poet's moral backbone finds a corollary in Gil de Biedma's attitude toward his craft. Like many other poets of the 1950s, the author of *Moralidades* shows little interest in forging an ostensibly beautiful poetic language. His diction is seemingly unremarkable and his tone is rarely ecstatically lyrical. Yet he is a virtuoso of poetic form, in both obvious and subtle ways. "Epístola francesa" ["French epistle"] (*Las personas del verbo*, 107), for example, is written in fairly fluent French alexandrine couplets that alternate between feminine and masculine rhymes.

The poem "Apología y petición" (82) is another tour de force. This poem is a sestina, a fixed form of Provençal origin, which is frequent in the poetry of W. H. Auden. It consists of six stanzas of six lines followed by a three line envoi; each line must end with a specific word according to a preset pattern. If the last words of each line in the first stanza are designated by numbers one through six, this pattern is as follows:

1 2 3 4 5 6 (stanza 1)
6 1 5 2 4 3
3 6 4 1 2 5
5 3 2 6 1 4
4 5 1 3 6 2
2 4 6 5 3 1
(1) 2 (3) 4 (5) 6 (envoi)

The numbers in parenthesis designate words in the middle of the last three lines of the poem. The first two stanzas of "Apología petición" demonstrate the beginning of this circular pattern:

> Y qué decir de nuestra madre España,
> este país de todos los demonios
> en donde el mal gobierno, la pobreza
> no son, sin más, pobreza y mal gobierno
> sino un estado místico del hombre,
> la absolución final de nuestra historia?
>
> De todas las historias de la Historia
> sin duda la más triste es la de España,
> porque termina mal. Como si el hombre,
> harto ya de luchar contra sus demonios,
> decidiese encargarles el gobierno
> y la administración de su pobreza.
>
> (*Las personas del verbo*, 82)

> And what can we say of our mother Spain,
> this country of all the demons
> where bad government and poverty
> are not simply poverty and bad government

but a mystical state of Man,
the final absolution of our history?

Of all the histories of History
without a doubt the saddest is that of Spain
because it ends badly. As if Man,
finally tired of struggling against his demons,
decided to entrust to them the government
and administration of his poverty.

Readers who do not notice (or who do not appreciate) the poem's fixed form are likely to remain rather unimpressed with it, reading it as a prosaic statement of political ideas. The students in my recent graduate seminar, in fact, were unfamiliar with the sestina form and did not notice the symmetrical recurrence of the six end words, although they did find the poem rather "repetitive." The literariness of the poem lies not in its verbal inventiveness or beauty, but in the virtuosity of the form itself and, more importantly, in the apparently arbitrary relation between the traditional form and the "social" statement it encloses: a condemnation of the contemporary political situation in Spain.

What is the role of the creative process in the elaboration of such a poem? At first glance it might seem that such an explicitly didactic statement belongs to the poetics of communication rather than the process oriented poetry of *conocimiento:* the poet appears to be simply transmitting his views of Spanish history and politics to the reader. Yet a writing process, of a very different sort, is actually intrinsic to the sestina form itself. Rather than choosing an open-ended form that follows the contours of his own thought, Gil de Biedma makes the arbitrary decision to follow a preestablished pattern and to see where it leads him. This initial decision does not imply that form can be completely separated from content. Instead, the sestina becomes a generative device that actually produces the content of the poem.[12]

After choosing his six initial words, the poet faces a formal problem that he can only solve by inventing ideas that conform to the preordained sequence of line endings. This sort of poetic process is quite dissimilar to the quasi-surrealist compository process of a work like Claudio Rodríguez's *Don de la ebriedad.* Gil de Biedma's philosophy of composition is more akin to Bertold Brecht's "estrangement effect," a technique that emphasizes the distance between form and content. Gil de Biedma's aesthetic, like that of Brecht, is antiorganicist; it is designed to provoke a questioning of conventional modes of thought that more natural seeming literary forms often reinforce.

Although some readers might object in principle to any separation of form and content, Gil de Biedma's text invites exactly this variety of dissociation. In spite of the closure implicit in the sestina form, with its fixed and circular form, the gap between "form" and "content" remains open to several interpretations. There are at least three approaches to the problem:

1. Form reflects content: the circular and repetitious sestina mirrors the cyclic fatalities of Spain history. This interpretation, favored by the majority of the students in my seminar, in effect "naturalizes" or justifies the relation of form to content.
2. Form opposes content in a parodic way. The use of the fixed form implies a critique of the tautological and formulaic discourse of Marxist discourse itself: language speaks the poet rather than the other way around. The conclusion of the sestina is completely preordained and predictable, in the same way that Marxist arguments are:

> Pido que España expulse a esos demonios.
> Que la pobreza suba hasta el gobierno.
> Que sea el hombre dueño de la historia.

>   (83)

> I ask that Spain expel those demons.
> That poverty rise up to the government.
> That man be the master of history.

   Words like *hombre* and *historia,* of course, form part of the standard rhetoric of the Spanish communist party.
3. Form and content go their separate ways. The cultured bourgeois "social" poet, bored with the task of communicating a political message in prosaic language, exercises his purely formal skill by fulfilling the requirements of a difficult troubador form.

The first approach satisfies the urge of the traditional literary critic to find some sort of correspondence between form and content. The second and third alternatives are more "deconstructive" in that they call into question the assumption that there is a natural relation between signifier and signified. My own preference is for the second, parodic reading. Rather than adjudicating between these divergent interpretations, however, I would suggest a metaliterary approach that incorporates them all: the poet's aim is to problematize the relation between content and expression and thereby to provoke an interrogation of the conventional opposition between politically committed poetry and aestheticism.

"El juego de hacer versos" ["The game of writing in verse"] is a more explicitly self-conscious statement of poetics than the ambiguous "Apología y petición." It is an *ars poetica* that is comparable to many other poems written by Gil de Biedma's contemporaries, such as Angel González's "Metapoesía" series, and José Angel Valente's *Mandorla*.[13] Gil de Biedma's justification of his art is quite different in tone from those of other poets of his generational group, primarily because his claims for the importance of poetry are much more modest. His deflation of the traditional values attributed to the poet's task is apparent from the first lines of the poem:

> El juego de hacer versos
> —que no es un juego—es algo
> parecido en principio
> al placer solitario.
>
> Con la primera muda,
> en los años nostálgicos
> de nuestra adolescencia,
> a escribir empezamos.
>
> Y son nuestros poemas
> del todo imaginarios
> —demasiado inexpertos
> ni siquiera plagiamos—
>
> porque la Poesía
> es un ángel abstracto
> y, como todos ellos,
> predispuesto a halagarnos.

El arte es otra cosa
distinta. El resultado
de mucha vocación
y un poco de trabajo.

Aprender a pensar
en renglones contados
—y no en los sentimientos
con que nos exaltábamos—

tratar con el idioma
como si fuera mágico
es un buen ejercicio
que llega a emborracharnos.

(*Las personas del verbo,* 138–39)

The game of writing in verse—
which is not a game—is something
in principle resembling
solitary pleasure.

With the first change of voice,
in the nostalgic years
of our adolescence,
we begin to write.

And our poems are
completely imaginary—
too unskilled
we don't even plagiarize—

because Poetry
is an abstract angel
and, like all the others,
is predisposed to flatter us.

Art is something else
entirely. The result
of a lot of vocation
and a little work.

To learn to think
in counted lines—
and not in the sentiments
with which we were exalted—

to treat language
as though it were magic
is a good exercise
that even intoxicates us.

The phrase "El juego de hacer versos" connotes technical skill rather than exalted poetic vision. Gil de Biedma ironically devalues the adolescent rapture that fails to produce a polished artistic artifact, establishing an opposition between "Poesía," capitalized as an abstract essence, and the lower case "arte," which in this context connotes careful craft. We might contrast Gloria Fuertes's attitude: "Técnica: (¡Qué aburrimiento!)" ["Technique: (What a bore!)"].[14] The idea of thinking in metrical form itself, in "renglones contados," rather than in emotions, implies that the poet must learn to discipline himself. The magic of words is illusory, an "as if" produced by poetic sleight of hand. Poetic drunkenness is the result of this technical effect; it is not the mystical state of inspiration seen in a work like Claudio Rodríguez's *Don de la ebriedad.*

In his rejection of a transcendental role for poetry Gil de Biedma emphasizes that more common-sense view that poetic language is a finely tuned instrument of communication:

Luego está el instrumento
en su punto afinado:
la mejor poesía
es el verbo hecho tango.

Y los poemas son
un modo que adoptamos
para que nos entiendan
y que nos entendamos.

(*Las personas del verbo,* 139)

Then the instrument is
finely tuned:
the best poetry
is the verb made a tango.

And poems are
a way that we adopt
so that we can be understood
and understand ourselves.

This definition of poetry's function contrasts with the more ambitious projects of Gil de Biedma's contemporaries. For Valente, for example, the poetic word is the dwelling place of infinite signification. It is traditional to contrast the linguistic faith of earlier twentieth-century writers with the more skeptical attitudes of the poets of the 1950s. For all their apparent distrust of language, however, Valente and Rodríguez never abandon their underlying faith in the word: they criticize inauthentic language, but only in order to make way for a more authentic *logos*. Authentic language might be an exceptional state of affairs, but it is this exception that justifies poetry. Gil de Biedma, in contrast, makes no transcendental claims for "Poesía" in this exalted sense.

After several additional stanzas, which list the major thematic preoccupations of Gil de Biedma's work, "El juego de hacer versos" concludes with a transformation of the initial stanza:

> El juego de hacer versos,
> que no es un juego, es algo
> que acaba pareciéndose
> al vicio solitario.
>
> (*Las personas del verbo*, 140)

> The game of writing in verse,
> which is not a game, is something
> that ends up resembling
> the solitary vice.

The more innocent childhood *placer* gives way to the adult poet's *vicio*. Gil de Biedma equates the writing of verse with masturbation. Once again, the contrast with the work of Valente and Rodríguez is evident. For the latter poets, writing is not a solitary vice but a fertile act of communion with the Other. Valente, for instance, defines artistic creation as a sexual act experienced from a "feminine" position: "no es acto de penetración de la materia, sino pasión de ser penetrado por ella" ["it is not an act of penetration of matter, but the passion of being penetrated by it"].[15] Rodríguez describes the poetic process as a "dissemination" of the poet's ego that produces the possibility of renewed life:

> Como si nunca hubiera sido mía
> dad al aire mi voz y que en el aire
> sea de todos y la sepan todos
> igual que una mañana o una tarde.[16]

> As if it had never been mine
> give my voice to the air and in the air
> let it belong to everyone and let everyone know it
> just like a morning or an afternoon.

Gil de Biedma values the ability of the conscious mind to control and evaluate experience, but this attitude, which I have provisionally termed "rationalism," puts little emphasis on *reason* per se. The sestina form appears coherent in its own terms but in no way ensures the ultimate rationality of the poem's discourse. Likewise, the poet's mastery of verse form, which for Yvor Winters would have symbolized his ability to evaluate experience in a rational and morally mature manner, is not actually identical with this ethical posture. Gil de Biedma's posture, then, is best defined as an anti-irrationalism, a distrust of the irrational powers of poetry celebrated by so many other modern and postmodern poets. In this respect, Gil de Biedma anticipates Guillermo Carnero, whose work self-consciously explores the inadequacy of reason to encompass reality. Both poets place a great degree of importance in the power of the human mind to order reality, while at the same time viewing this order as a fundamentally arbitrary one.

The most salient feature of Gil de Biedma's poetics is his distrust of the irrationalism that has dominated much modern and contemporary poetry. From romanticism to the present day, the celebration of irrationality has given the poet an oracular, quasi-religious stature. Examples include Yeats's experiments with mysticism, Rilke's use of the Orpheus myth, Neruda's prophetic voice, and Wallace Stevens's view of poetry as a replacement for religion. In a more immediate context, Gil de Biedma's own cohorts are heirs to this tradition. José Angel Valente's abiding interest in the language of mysticism, and his disdain for instrumental language, provides the clearest instance of the continued reliance on this exalted view of poetic language. Jaime Gil de Biedma, in contrast, emphasizes verse-craftsmanship and the ability to see his own life in lucid terms. His more matter-of-fact anti-irrationalism thus deflates traditional claims for the transcendent significance of the poet's art.

7

Postmodernism, Culturalism, Kitsch

I. The *Novísimos:* Culture and Counterculture

The most striking feature of Spanish poetry in the 1970s is its "culturalismo": an obsessive and at times excessive citation of artistic and literary intertexts. The abundance of proper names and foreign-language quotations immediately identifies the poems of the *novísimos,* the group of poets who first came into the public eye in José María Castellet's polemical 1970 anthology.[1] The culturalism of these poets is so self-evident that critics have not felt the need to analyze it: they have used the concept primarily as a way of defining the *novísimos* as a "generation," distinct from both older and younger poets.

Culturalist intertextuality is clearly related to another of the defining characteristics of the *novísimos:* the practice of metapoetry. The citation of intertexts serves to flaunt the literariness of the poem. The text's referents are other texts and thus, directly or indirectly, its own textuality. Such poetry shuts itself off from reality, or, more accurately, redefines "reality" itself as a fabric of cultural texts. This is a significant development in the context of post–Spanish Civil War poetry: until the late 1960s, the majority of poets emphasized the non- or even antiliterary nature of poetry, its rejection of artificial conventions. The proponents of "social poetry" dominated public discourse about poetry from the 1940s to the 1960s. Poets of the so-called "second generation" of the postwar period, although they rejected the social-realist aesthetic, continued to stress the connection between language and experience. The young poets of 1970 are the first since the war to privilege the distance between literary conventions and social reality in an explicit way.

The culturalism of the *novísimos*, nevertheless, is also a counter-culturalism, a critical reevaluation of the tradition of Western civilization that they have inherited. In the first place, they show a deliberate preference for texts that are *marginal* rather than central to this tradition. Relatively minor figures are often preferred to canonical landmarks. Historical figures marginalized from their own society—social pariahs, homosexuals, *poètes maudits*, mad-men, avant-garde writers—all exercise a particular fascination. Spanish writers take a decidedly secondary place to foreigners.

This taste for the exotic, the minor, and the marginal serves to differentiate the "culturalismo" of the *novísimos* from the intertextuality of older poets. The social poet Blas de Otero, for example, frequently cites the central texts of the Western and the Hispanic tradition: the Bible, *El Cid*, and *Don Quijote*. He takes advantage of the prestige traditionally attributed to these texts in order to lend rhetorical force to his own position. Spanish poets of the 1960s and 1970s, in contrast, often call into question the value of the received culture. In the "countercultural" atmosphere of the times, even extremely well-read writers express an irreverent attitude toward the literary and artistic past. Without directly advocating book burning, several have toyed with the idea. Antonio Martínez Sarrión concludes his "Fuegos artificales" [Fireworks], a collage of cultural intertexts, with the line "se está quemando toda la CULTURA"[2] ["All CULTURE is burning up"]. Pepe Carvalho, a detective appearing in a series of novels by Manuel Vázquez Montalbán, uses volumes from his extensive library to start his fireplace.

It could be argued that the culturalism of the *novísimos*, in spite of its subversion of aesthetic hierarchies, does indeed frequently reinforce the prestige traditionally attached to high culture. The apparent inconsistency here is due, in part, to differences of attitude between individual poets. A poet such as Antonio Colinas, who was not included in Castellet's *Nueve novísimos*, tends to employ cultural monuments of the past in order to demonstrate the permanence of artistic traditions. Guillermo Carnero also privileges high culture, seldom mentioning the products of popular or mass art. It could also be argued that frequent allusions to "minor" figures, instead of subverting the canon, actually allow its center to remain undisturbed. The erudition of the younger poets of the 1960s and 1970s—many of whom are now university professors—is often impressive. When Carnero's poetry appears to apologize for his recondite taste in music—"También nos duele confesar / una secreta admiración por Donizetti" ["It is also painful to confess / our secret admiration for Donizetti"—the reader can assume a wide knowledge of the more canonical figures of occidental music.[3] His gesture is quite distinct from Luis Cernuda's homage to Mozart in *La desolación de la quimera:* "Mozart / Es la gloria de Europa, el ejemplo más alto / De la gloria del mundo, porque Europa es el mundo"[4] ["Mozart / Is Europe's glory, the highest example / Of the world's glory, for Europe is the world"]. In contrast to Cernuda's unabashedly Eurocentric affirmation, Carnero implies that listening to Donizetti and other analogous activities have a decidedly minor role to play in contemporary society. Still, Carnero does not question the centrality of European culture.

Many of the younger poets of the late sixties and early seventies remain ambivalent about the very idea of "culture": they neither burn the library nor assume its permanent relevance. Their transformation of cultural intertexts can best be characterized as an alternation between a revindication of popular culture and an ironic misappropriation of high culture. "Camp" employs citation in order to produce a vicarious aesthetic effect. Works like Ana María Moix's *Baladas del dulce Jim* (1969), Leopoldo María Panero's *Así se fundó Carnaby Street* (1970), and Pedro Gimferrer's *La muerte en Beverly Hills* (1967) create collages of references to popular culture, especially American gangster movies, in order to suggest an ambience of dreamlike unreality. In such works, the stereotyped images of mass culture mask the experience of the lyric subject: the poet refracts his or her own vision through a repertoire of culturally defined clichés. "Cuando amanezca me encontrarán muerto y llamarán a Charlie Chan"[5] ["When dawn breaks they'll find me dead and call in Charlie Chan"].

The citation of "high" cultural artifacts also creates a vicarious aesthetic effect. The self-consciously aestheticist posture of the *novísimos* remains controversial today, for it deliberately inverts one of the principal tenets of postwar Spanish poetry: the devaluation of artistic refinement per se in the name of social utility and humanist values. The beauty that they attempt to evoke in their poems, however, derives in large measure from the description of stereotypically exquisite settings: the refinement of eighteenth-century court society or the decadent art-for-art's-sake of the fin de siècle. Venice is a favorite locale among these poets, prompting some to call them the "Venetian" school. This tendency can come dangerously close to "kitsch," the polar opposite of camp. While camp attributes aesthetic value to popular forms that snobs have traditionally disdained, kitsch attempts to borrow its aesthetic prestige from a previously accepted aesthetic tradition. In their evocation of atmospheres that are already culturally defined as beautifully artistic, it could be argued that the *novísimos* recycle late nineteenth-century aestheticism rather than creating an original aesthetic sensibility of their own.

While conceding that the *novísimos* descend to kitsch on occasion, I would attribute this critique to a sort of optical illusion resulting from an overgeneralized vision of their generational project. The impression that these poets are practicing a sterile aestheticism tends to dissipate in the examination of individual poems. What often saves them from the second-hand aestheticism of kitsch is their self-conscious transformation of borrowed material. In their best and most characteristic work, they do not simply assume the value of cultural citations, but rather deploy them as pre-texts for further metapoetic explorations, consciously exploring the vicariousness inherent in any literary or artistic representation.

The choice of intertexts, along with the particular use to which they are put, reveals the poet's particular vision of language, poetry, and culture. The rise of culturalism in Spanish poetry toward the end of the sixties can be explained in sociopolitical and "cultural" terms as the reaction of a better-educated younger generation against the artistic poverty of the postwar period. After a certain point, however, generalization about "culturalism" brings diminished returns, since poets of radically different sensibilities have practiced the poetics of cultural intertextuality. Manuel Vázquez Montalbán and Antonio Martínez Sarrión allude to the popular culture of the Franco era in order to unmask the falsity of Spanish society. Marcos Ricardo Barnatán, born in Argentina but residing in Spain, explores attitudes toward language derived from the traditions of Jewish mysticism. Antonio Colinas identifies the "eternal themes" of his own work in the age-old cultural traditions of the mediterranean region.

In the second and third sections of this chapter, I investigate two versions of culturalism: the intellectual metapoetry of Guillermo Carnero and the postmodern nostalgia of José María Alvarez. A final section takes up the work of the most recent generation of Spanish poets, whose culturalism differs from that of the *novísimos* in both intensity and intention.

II. Guillermo Carnero: Ideas of Order

Guillermo Carnero, one of the most self-conscious poets among the *novísimos*, explores the relation between language and reality in an intellectually rigorous way. The culturalist intertexts that appear in his work function primarily as models of artistic order: he employs these previous attempts to impose a rational structure on a chaotic reality as metaphors for his own poetic task. Carnero views rationality itself as irrational. This paradox results from his realization that the structure of human knowledge and language are arbitrary constructions that are incommensurate with reality itself. In spite of the arbitrariness of rationality, the impulse to give shape to experience is unavoidable. Art may be inadequate as a representation of reality, but it is the only means available. The limitations of the human mind doom the task of ordering reality to perpetual failure. At the same time, however, the arbitrariness of such attempts allows the artist the freedom to create new meaning out of chaos. The crisis of rationality thus highlights the status of art as a medium for the fictive ordering of reality.

Carnero's early poems, collected in *Dibujo de la muerte* [Drawing of death] (1967), establish the central opposition between vitality and art that will persist in a different form in the later, more overtly intellectual, poetry of *Variaciones y figuras sobre un tema de La Bruyère* [Variations and figures on a theme by La Bruyère] (1974) and *El azar objetivo* [Objective chance] (1975).[6] The early Carnero is less preoccupied with rationality per se: he identifies the force that represses life not with reason but with aestheticism, an attitude that privileges elegance over vital exuberance. In poems such as "Capricho en Aranjuez," the overabundance of decorative details oppresses the individual. The first line of this poem, "Raso amarillo a cambio de mi vida" ["Yellow satin in exchange for my life"], sharply establishes the opposition between external elegance and vitality. The aestheticism of Carnero's own elegant verse, then, unmasks its own superficiality. Poems that have been read as expressions of cultural snobbism are actually ironical condemnations of this very attitude.[7] Angel González's parody of the *novísimos*, "Oda a los nuevos bardos" ["Ode to the new bards"], concludes with a line that echoes Carnero's condemnation of empty elegance: "Pesados terciopelos sus éxtasis sofocan" ["Heavy velvet suffocates their ecstasies"].[8] This explicit critique of Carnero's aestheticism misses the mark somewhat, since Carnero himself portrays the figure of the elegant dandy in a negative light.

The poem "Eupalinos," the fifth section of *El azar objetivo*, exemplifies Carnero's use of cultural intertexts as "ideas of order." As the perhaps oxymoronic title of this short sequence of poems suggests, his main concern is the conflict between chaotic chance and the seemingly objective rationality of human reason. As Mirta Camandone de Cohen puts it, "El azar se adueña de la realidad, destruyendo los penosos intentos clasificadores. La racionalización es inútil porque la realidad sólo finge espejismos"[9] ["Chance takes control of reality, destroying the painful attempts at classification. Rationality is futile because reality only presents mirages"]. I follow this critic as well as Carlos Bousoño in interpreting Carnero's enterprise as a "burla de la razón" [parody of reason] rather than an affirmation of the ideal of objectivity. (*Ensayo*, 66–67).

The opening lines of the poem are difficult to interpret without the context provided by the poem that precedes it in *El azar objetivo*, "Elogio de la dialéctica a la manera de Magritte" ["Praise of dialectics à la Magritte"]. My analysis begins, then, with the concluding lines from this poem:

Y bien, cuando los contempla fijamente le huyen,
y en el brillo lustroso con que aquel ir y venir los decora
además de afirmarse, aún provocan a risa
pero no a él, pues es risa de las superficies rotundas
dando fe del volumen que a pesar suyo exhiben;

por más que el procedimiento se le revele inane
persiste, que aunque estéril es al cabo seguro.

(191)

Fine, but when he stares at them they escape his fixed gaze,
and in the polished gleam that adorns them as they come and go
affirming themselves, they still provoke laughter
but not from him, for it is the laughter of the rounded surfaces
testifying to the volume they exhibit without wanting to;
no matter how inane this procedure seems to him
he persists, for although sterile, it is in the end certain.

The antecedent of the pronoun *los* in the first line quoted here is "los objetos," objects which the unnamed male individual is attempting to subject to an objective gaze. The dry, pseudotechnical language of this passage is a parody of the discourse of academic objectivity. The unheroic protagonist of the poem himself finds his own solution to the problem of perception absurd, but he persists in his sterile and safe method.

"Eupalinos" begins with a potential objection, posed by the readers of the poem, to the protagonist's rational and life-denying gaze, followed by the narrator's extended answer:

Luego—decís—la contemplación de ese menguado tesoro
le niega la vida real—
               Más bien él la convierte,
de propia elección, en un estercolero,
propiciado por tal epistemología de la basura;
en efecto, la contempla como desde una altura excesiva,
con supresión de todo oído y tacto,
veía Fabrizio pasar los bueyes de reata,
abejas de oro sobre las páginas de un salterio,
con ese color miel pulido por la distancia;
la contempla para irle robando como un entomólogo de opereta
imágenes ligeras y fantasmas aéreos,
fragmentos de porcelana, alfileres, medallas, los cuales
son, mucho después, en la soledad de su mente
una vida de mayor alcance.

(192)

"Therefore," you say, "to contemplate this diminished treasure
is to deny it real life."
               Instead he transforms it,
through his own decision, into a dungheap,
encouraged by such an epistemology of garbage;

in fact, he contemplates it as from an excessive height,
suppressing all hearing and touch,
Fabrizio saw a string of oxen pass by,
golden bees on the pages of a psalter,
with that color of honey polished by distance;
he contemplates it in order to steal from it, like an entomologist
    in an operetta,
light images and air-borne fantasies,
fragments of porcelain, stick-pins, medals,
all of which are, much later, in the solitude of his mind
a life of greater dimensions.

The speaker of the poem argues for the possible benefits of the protagonist's objective vision of reality, in an attempt to redeem this vision from the accusation of sterility. Instead of simply denying vitality, this vision transforms its objects into a fertile source of contemplation by means of an "epistemología de la basura." This phrase implies that reality itself is worthless, and that the best way of studying it is from a great distance: accuracy of perception results not from the object itself but from the power of the mind to create its own structures. Sight, significantly, suppresses the other senses, which are traditionally considered less purely intellectual.

Two entomologists, one serious and one comic, exemplify the distanced mode of vision. Fabrizio perceives the oxen, from a distance, as if they were letters of a book, thus transforming brute reality into written text.[10] The "entomólogo de opereta" is a stock comic figure whose pursuit of butterflies leaves him unfit for a more practical existence. In spite of his ethereal view of reality, however, the protagonist is able to reorder the data of his perception in order to construct "una vida de mayor alcance" in his memory.

In the next section of the poem the narrator suggests the possibility that a more fruitful vision will result from an imaginative re-creation of this raw data. The still-fertile seeds found in the tomb of an ancient Egyptian queen symbolize the miraculous power of human architecture to preserve life:

En la tumba de Hatshepsuth
se encontró entre el ajuar funerario
una veintena de granos de trigo
con aptitud germinativa.

Eupalinos
alzó su templete redondo sobre cuatro columnas,
imagen matemática de una muchacha de Corinto:
no cuestiona él la legitimidad del procedimiento
puesto que no se le alcanza alternativa posible
pero obtiene con ello mayor nitidez
en las imágenes (y una mayor gratificación afectiva,
pues les da mayor nitidez—
                                        existencia
equivale a gratificación afectiva
acompañada de mayor nitidez—
                                        ordena el caos
de la vida real, tan inferior a su memoria,
le confiere sentido y mayor nitidez.

                                                        (192)

In Hatshepsuth's tomb
they found in the funeral trousseau
some twenty wheat seeds
that could still germinate.
                                Eupalinos
built his round temple on four columns,
a mathematical image of a Corinthian girl:
he doesn't question the legitimacy of this procedure
since no other possible alternative is within his reach
but he obtains with it a greater sharpness
in the images (and a greater affective gratification
since it gives them greater sharpness)—
                                        existence
is equivalent to affective gratification
accompanied by greater sharpness—
                                        he orders the chaos
of real life, so inferior to his memory,
he endows it with sense and greater sharpness.

The culminating image that gives the poem its title, Eupalinos's temple, derives from Paul Valéry's Platonic dialogue "Eupalinos, ou l'architecte," written and published in 1921. The passage that serves as Carnero's immediate inspiration reads as follows:

Où le passant ne voit qu'une élégante chapelle,—c'est peu de chose: quatre colonnes, un style très simple,—j'ai mis le souvenir d'un clair jour de ma vie. O douce métamorphose! Ce temple délicat, nul ne le sait, est l'image mathématique d'une fille de Corinthe, que j'ai heureusement aimée. Il en reproduit fidèlement les proportions particulières. Il vit pour moi! Il me rend ce que je lui ai donné.[11]

Where the passerby sees only an elegant chapel,—it is an insignificant thing: four columns, a very simple style,—I have placed the memory of a bright day of my life. Oh sweet metamorphosis! This delicate temple, nobody knows it, is the mathematical image of a Corinthian girl, whom I happily loved. It faithfully reproduces her particular proportions. It lives for me! It gives me back what I have given it.

Valéry's dialogue touches upon many of the themes that preoccupy Carnero, including the relation between reality and art, the imposition of form on chaos, and the use of art as a way of commemorating past life. The speaker of this passage, the architect Eupalinos, has translated a memory of the Corinthian girl into the ordered, mathematical structure of his temple through the sweet metamorphosis of art. In Carnero's poem this image carries more emotional weight than the anecdote of the seeds. Eupalinos has constructed the exact mathematical equivalent of his human love, but the connection between the girl and the temple is pathetically tenuous.

The conclusion of "Eupalinos" seems anticlimactic in tone. After presenting several aesthetically satisfying and emotionally charged images, the poem resumes with the dry, abstractly philosophical style seen in "Elogio de la dialéctica." Prosaic constructions and technical-sounding phrases serve to distance the protagonist's emotion.[12] The clinical phrase "gratificación afectiva," for example, denotes a feeling of emotional pleasure without evoking a parallel reaction in the reader. In this way the speaker's language demonstrates the very theory of objective vision that the poem proposes.

The poem ends with an obsessive reaffirmation of the value of "nitidez": clarity of perception takes precedence over the messy vitality of the "estercolero." It is clear that there is no alternative to this distanced vision: "puesto que no se le alcanza alternativa posible." A vital participation in life is no longer a viable option for the protagonist of the poem, since his life has already taken the form of a lifeless memory. His choice to see reality as garbage allows him to transform this memory into a clear-cut artistic structure like that of Eupalinos's temple. Any other decision would be less satisfactory than his lifeless yet artistically fertile vision of reality.

The paradox of Carnero's poetry is that it clings relentlessly to the very values that it parodies. The self-conscious aestheticism of his earlier poetry has a largely negative connotation: the aesthete is captive in an artificial world of beauty that represses his or her desire for a more authentic existence. By the same token, the philosophical rigor of *El azar objetivo* and other later works is belied by the poet's ultimate skepticism. A reader who shares Carnero's own disdain for objectivity and rationality might not be interested in following the steps of his intricate pseudorational arguments.

Carnero's stated opinion on the question of metapoetry helps to explain this paradox: "no puede haber metapoesía si no hay poesía primero, es decir, si las cuestiones reflexivas no están emocionalmente interiorizadas, si no responden a una problemática personal" [There can be no metapoetry unless there is poetry first, that is to say, unless the reflexive issues are emotionally internalized, unless they respond to a personal problematic].[13] Carnero's metapoetic discourse, then, consists of a secondary discourse that reflects upon the original emotional impulse. Rather than evoking emotion in a direct way, Carnero conceals it beneath an excessively rational discourse. The repression of this original emotion produces a secondary emotion, a feeling of loss that occurs as the poet encloses himself completely within an arbitrary artistic order. The emotion conveyed to the reader, then, results from the poignant contrast between an excessive rationality and the affective content that it represses.

Carnero's use of culturalist intertexts, past models of artistic order, forms part of his strategy of concealing the emotional impact of his poetry behind a metapoetic discourse. He shows a particular preference for the eighteenth century, which is both the age of courtly elegance and of enlightenment reason. (As an academic scholar, he has written extensively on eighteenth-century Spanish literature.) His identification with his precursor texts, however, is primarily parodic, given his postmodern skepticism about language and its capacity to deal with the world in reasonable terms. His real affinities lie with the postenlightenment crisis of reason that manifests itself in postmodern philosophy.

The notion that the artist must give order to reality is reminiscent of the literary modernism of Wallace Stevens. Where Guillermo Carnero's "ideas of order" diverge from those of his modernist precursor is in their extreme arbitrariness and contingency. The author of *El azar objetivo* uses past models of artistic order in a primarily ironical fashion, as if to suggest that the age in which such models were truly viable is long past.

III. José María Alvarez: Postmodernism as Cultural Nostalgia

> Joya de esa memoria
> que con el pasado nos consuela,
> entre ésas, pocas, imágenes
> que rezumadas por el tiempo
> se revelan los más precisos símbolos
> de lo que fue nuestro deseo . . .[14]

> The jewel of that memory
> which consoles us for the past,
> among those few images
> seeping from time
> that are revealed: the most precise symbols
> of what our desire once was . . .

No one better deserves the "culturalist" label than José María Alvarez, whose monumental *Museo de cera* [Wax museum] contains more allusions per page than that of any poet since Ezra Pound.[15] At times the sheer density of quotation threatens to overwhelm Alvarez's individual poetic voice. The poems in *Museo* are organized into three books of three chapters each. Each book and chapter is headed by several epigraphs. In a similar fashion, each poem begins with a title, normally an allusion of some sort, and one or more additional epigraphs and dedications. The body of the poem will typically contain several more allusions. Even the book's table of contents has several epigraphs. The reader opening the 1978 edition of the book has occasion to peruse some fifteen quotations, by writers such as Kafavy (quoted in the original Greek), Melville, Shakespeare, Cernuda, Foucault, and Malcolm Lowry, before coming upon the poet's first "original" words.

In addition to the sheer number of intertexts, the brevity and slightness of many of Alvarez's poems make his original contribution to the wax museum seem relatively minimal. As Thomas

Franz noted in his review of the 1974 edition: "On some pages the poet's own compositions frankly pale alongside the quoted matter." [16] Often these poems portray the poet-speaker in a state of depression, ennui, drunkenness, or bile: "Luminosamente borracho y homicida"[17] ["Lucidly drunk and murderous"]. His favored intertexts, many derived from modern North American literature, music, and popular music, serve as touchstones, pretexts for an ironical and at times sarcastic reflection on his own situation. One problem for the reader of Alvarez's work is to disentangle the relation between the pretexts and the poet's gloss. This can be a difficult task, since many of the citations can only be understood in their original contexts. Often the connection is oblique or opaque, existing only as a private association. In Franz's view, "The quotes, while often giving the appearance of epigraphs, seem only occasionally related to the original matter on the same pages. They appear, rather, as independent, additional poems within the 'wax museum.'"[18]

Although his poetry is not as linguistically self-conscious as that of Carnero, Alvarez's characteristic collage technique does imply a particular theory of poetry. In the first place, the idea of the poet's original, unique voice has a less important role. The value of this poetry, such as it is, depends on Alvarez's ability to organize and manipulate the fragments of the cultural tradition. This task is similar to that undertaken by modernist poets such as T. S. Eliot and Ezra Pound, who created intertextual collages in *The Waste Land* and *The Cantos*, respectively. In "Tradition and Individual Talent," Eliot affirms that each major poet redefines the existing tradition: "The existing monuments form an ideal order among themselves, which is modified by the introduction of the new (the really new) work of art among them."[19] Eliot's struggle to create a space for his own work within the poetic tradition was largely successful, to the extent that his work affected the way in which critics viewed the history of English and American poetry. As Clement Greenberg notes, "with only a relatively small lapse of time the innovations of Modernism begin to look less and less radical, and . . . they almost all settle into place eventually as part of the continuum of high Western art, along with Shakespeare's verse and Rembrandt's drawing."[20]

Alvarez's project for a culturalist wax museum is less ambitious than that of Eliot's in several respects. In Eliot's conception of the relation of tradition to individual talent, the strength of a new poetic voice allows it not only to take its place alongside other canonical works, but also to modify the entire canon. Alvarez does create a highly personal anthology of intertexts (one that I hesitate to call a canon), but he does not strive to equal his masters or place his own efforts on the same level. This cannot be viewed as a shortcoming on the part of the Spanish poet, since Alvarez is conscious of living in an age in which Eliot's idea of the canon is no longer tenable. It is not simply that Alvarez is not as great a literary creator as the precursors whose cultural icons he preserves: it is the very nature of the enterprise that is different.

Although Alvarez's use of cultural citation can be traced to that of Eliot and Pound, a more immediate cultural context is the postmodern American poetry that derives from Poundian collage.[21] Critics have used the term *postmodernism* to refer to the work of several contemporary Spanish poets, but they have not compared these poets to postmodern poets outside of Spain. To speak of "postmodernism" in contemporary Spanish poetry is to translate, to employ a term in a cultural context that is different from that in which it originated. The word itself originated in American literature, where it was used by the poet Charles Olson in the 1950s.[22] The group of poets who came of age in 1950s and were included in Donald Allen's 1960 anthology, *The New American Poetry*, includes many followers of Olson, along with the so-called New York poets (John Ashbery, Frank O'Hara, Kenneth Koch), the Beat Generation (Allen Ginsberg, Gregory Corso), and the San Francisco Renaissance (Robert Duncan, Jack Spicer).[23] These poets represent the enormous vitality of the alternative, nonacademic, current of postwar American poetry. Most were born in the midtwenties and produced their most important work during the fifties and early sixties.[24]

In Spain, postmodern poetry occurs as a belated movement. The poets who are most directly comparable to those of *The New American Poetry* are those of Alvarez's generation, who come of age in the late 1960s. Born in the late thirties to midforties, these poets average twenty years younger than their American counterparts. José María Castellet's *Nueve novísimos poetas españoles* was published ten years after *The New American Poetry*. There is some evidence that the *novísimos* and other poets of the same age are familiar with the poets included in Don Allen's anthology. Marcos Ricardo Barnatán, for example, has translated and anthologized the poets of the Beat Generation. More important than the direct *influence* of American poetry, however, is the fact that the two groups are framed within a common matrix, that they respond to similar cultural stimuli. What is most significant is that the young Spanish poets of 1970 come of age in a cultural context already defined, at least in part, by the postmodern poets in the United States. The interest among Spanish poets in the popular culture of the United States is marked. Hollywood movies occupy a privileged space in their imagination, as does jazz. The "camp" sensibility of the *novísimos* has often been noted. On the level of "high" culture, the resurgence of interest in the great modern poets, and in the historical avant-garde, is a common denominator among "postmoderns" of both nations. Both groups of poets saw themselves as the revindicators of the achievements of the great figures of the 1920s, in opposition to the aesthetically unadventurous "academic" poetry of the immediate postwar years.

It is difficult to generalize on the basis of one-to-one comparisons between individual poets. Nevertheless, Frank O'Hara, a major American poet of this period, is an interesting precursor of Alvarez's method. A juxtaposition of poems by Alvarez and O'Hara will highlight the similar way the two poets make use of cultural intertextuality:

CRISTALERÍA DE SEDA

Mi relato será fiel a la realidad o, en todo caso, a mi
recuerdo personal de la realidad, lo cual, es lo mismo.
—Jorge Luis Borges

A
Txaro Santoro

Escucho el Trio N. 6 para piano violín
y violonchello en Si bemol mayor
de Beethoven Miro
los retratos de Borges y de Shakespeare
que me miran
Tengo en mis

manos una
pitillera de plata que compré
a un anticuario de Istanbul
su anagrama bellísimo
GL Quién y cuándo
con cuánto amor encargaría
esta pieza
Y aquél para quien iba destinada
                              Deseo
seguir bebiendo Deseo
leer de nuevo a Conrad

                    Unos metros
debajo de mis pies
hace 2600 años hombres que venían del mar levantaron
a otros dioses un templo

                    Y hay serenas
madrugadas en que la noche restituye
murallas heladas
barcos de oro y puertos sumergidos
viejas canciones de Fenicia.
Ni una piedra siquiera
de tantas puertas como tomé
cubrirá mi memoria
                    En esta hora
engaño ya no cabe
Sino firme
gesto y sereno pensamiento
                    Mi linaje
no aplacará rigores de otro César

Sé lo que nunca
he de tener La página
que nunca será escrita
La mujer que nunca será amada
Los afectos perdidos

                    Silencioso
                              afilo
una espada
que también la muerta detendrá

Al tiempo que ha pasado por mi cuerpo
madurándolo abriéndolo
a la sabiduría amor belleza

encomiendo esta hora

Acepto

(*Museo de cera*, 168–69.)

SILK GLASS

My story will be faithful to reality or, in any case, to my personal memory of reality, which is the same thing.

—Jorge Luis Borges

To
Txaro Santoro

I listen to the Trio #6 for piano violin
and cello in B flat major
by Beethoven I look
at portraits of Borges and Shakespeare
looking back at me.
I hold in my
hands a
silver cigarette case I bought
from an antique seller in Istanbul
its beautiful initials
GL Who and when
with how much sentiment must have commissioned
this piece
And the one for whom it was meant.

I desire
to keep drinking I desire
to reread Conrad

A few meters
beneath my feet
2,600 years ago men from the sea erected
a temple to other gods.
And there are calm
early mornings when night restores
frozen ramparts
golden ships and sunken ports
old Phoenician songs
Not a single stone
from all the doors I've taken
will cover my memory
In this hour
there's no place for deceit

only firm
gestures and serene thoughts
                                        My lineage
will not appease the severity of another Caesar

I know what
I'm never meant to have The page
that will never be written
The woman who'll never be loved
The lost affections
                         Silently
                                   I hone
a sword
that death will also stop

To the time that has passed over my body
maturing it opening it
to wisdom love beauty
I dedicate this hour

                         I accept

Alvarez's degree of familiarity with O'Hara's work has no effect
on my argument, since coincidence can sometimes be more revealing that direct influence. Alvarez's poem, written some
twenty years after O'Hara's, reads like an imitation of the New
York poet's "I do this; I do that" mode, exemplified by "Getting
Up Before Someone (Sun)":

I cough a lot (sinus?) so I
get up and have some tea with cognac
it is dawn
              the light flows evenly along the lawn
in chilly Southampton and I smoke
and hours and hours go by I read
van Vechten's *Spider Boy* then a short
story by Patsy Southgate and poem
by myself it is cold and I shiver a little
in white shorts the day begun
so oddly not tired not nervous I
am for once truly awake letting it all
start slowly as I watch instead of
grabbing on late as usual
                              where did it go
                              it's not really awake yet

>   I will wait
> and the house gets up and goes
> to get the dog in Sag Harbor I make
> myself a bourbon and commence
> to write one of my "I do this I do that"
> poems in a sketch pad
>   it is tomorrow
> though only six hours have gone by
> each day's light has more significance these days[25]

Both Alvarez and O'Hara situate themselves personally within a context defined in terms of cultural icons—portraits, quotations, works of art. The insignificant, second-hand nature of these icons is in itself significant: in "Cristalería de seda" the portraits of Shakespeare and Borges, along with the recording of Beethoven, are mechanically reproduced artifacts. In both poems the speaker sets up an ironic contrast between the casual mode of present writing—both are drinking heavily—and traditional claims of poetic permanence. Both implicitly refute the idea that the lyric poem preserves the eternal moment of the poet's inspiration, that art is a defense against mortality. In both poems, the use of enjambment produces an effect of studied casualness. The postmodern poet, in contrast to the lyric poet in the traditional sense, lives day-by-day or moment-by-moment. Surrounded my mementoes of the past, he acknowledges that traditional claims of immortalization through artistic representation are illusory.

The speaker of "Getting up Ahead of Someone (Sun)" is concerned with capturing a moment of lyric consciousness as it passes. The traditional lyric epiphany, however, slips through his fingers in the very act of writing the poem we are now reading. O'Hara demonstrates the impossibility of the "eternal present" of lyric poetry by calling attention to the disparity between the time of writing and the time of experience: "it is tomorrow / though only six hours have gone by." In the more traditional lyric poem, these two moments are identified: the present tense refers both to the moment of writing and the lyric instant that the poem recreates. A similar moment of self-reflexivity occurs at the end of "Heart of Darkness," a poem from Alvarez's *El escudo de Aquiles* [The shield of Achilles]:

>   . . . Entonces,
> despacio, te sirves una copa, enciendes

> un cigarro, metes una cinta
> con "La Traviata", te sientas ante tu mesa
> y empiezas a escribir este poema.[26]

>   . . . Then,
> slowly, you pour yourself a drink, light
> a cigarette, put in a tape
> of "La Traviata," sit down at your table
> and begin to write this poem.

"Cristalería de seda" seems to have been written in a single time and place, but the table of contents reveals that the scene of writing is divided between two cities: "Cartagena–Madrid, marzo de 1977" (*Museo de cera*, 323).

The differences between Alvarez's and O'Hara's versions of postmodernism are as significant as the similarities. Alvarez is more concerned with canonical monuments of Western culture—Shakespeare, Beethoven, Conrad—whereas O'Hara's readings are more minor and eccentric: Patsy Southgate (a personal friend of the poet), Van Vechten (a relatively forgotten writer of the 1920s), and "a poem / by myself." Alvarez is more nostalgic, more oriented toward the past, as is evident in his archeological imagery. O'Hara appears to dwell entirely in the present moment; he is more aggressively postmodern in his disregard for the past. In a short, humorous piece entitled simply "Poem," O'Hara imagines the present in archeological terms:

> Some days I feel that I exude a fine dust
> like that attributed to Pylades in the famous
> *Chronica nera areopagitica* when it was found
> and it's because an excavationist has
> reached the inner chamber of my heart
> and rustled the paper bearing your name
>
> I don't like that stranger sneezing over our love[27]

The use of the archeological simile is highly ironic, since the dust that has accumulated on the speaker's love affair is relatively recent. Alvarez's contrast between himself and the ancient Phoenicians who inhabited his native Cartagena ("Carthago Nova") points to a more tragic understanding of the gap between past and present: "Mi linaje / no aplacará rigores de otro César." This gap is demonstrated in the poet's speculation on the mysterious initials found on his cigarette case. Future generations, perhaps, will read his poetry in the same way that he attempts to make sense of these signs, which have lost their connection to their original context and thus their communicative power. O'Hara, in contrast, seems less intent on deciphering the meanings of his magic charms in "Personal Poem":

> Now when I walk around at lunchtime
> I have only two charms in my pocket
> an old Roman coin Mike Kanemitsu gave me
> and a bolt-head that broke off a packing case
> when I was in Madrid . . .[28]

The preceding analysis of poems by Alvarez and O'Hara might serve as a basis for a historicist definition of postmodernism in contemporary Spanish poetry. This definition differs from the attempts of other critics to describe postmodernism as a form of textual indeterminacy. The problem with this approach, in my view, is that it robs postmodernism of its historical specificity: reader response and poststructuralist criticism will produce similar results with texts that predate the postmodern, or even the modern period. Readings that apply deconstructive theory to literary texts of any epoch will inevitably encounter indeterminacy and linguistic self-consciousness, since deconstruction is a theory of language rather than a theory of literary evolution. I would prefer to call these retrospective readings of older texts *poststructuralist*, reserving the *postmodern* label for texts that reflect a particular historical and cultural situation.

A strictly historicist definition of postmodernism would limit the phenomenon to that which comes after something called *modernism*—a term that is almost as difficult to define with precision. Postmodern poets rethink the modernity of modern poetry, and they do so by defining their own voices within a specific cultural context, defined by quotations from Borges, posters of Shakespeare, and short stories by Patsy Southgate. My time-bound reading of postmodernism takes into account the poets' own vision of history, of their own place within temporality. (The words *modernism* and *postmodernism*, after all, are both *period* terms.) Linda Hutcheon has spoken of the prototypical postmodern novel as "historiographic metafiction."[29] I would define postmodern poetry as historiographic metapoetry: poetry that is self-consciously concerned with defining its own place within history, although "history" in this case is mainly limited to particular literary, artistic, and cultural traditions. The preoccupation with the relation between past and present, present and future, marks the postmodern awareness of both José María Alvarez and Frank O'Hara.

Spanish postmodernism is further complicated by its belatedness, its post-postmodernity. Alvarez, obsessed by cultural memory, is already a second-generation postmodernist whose work echoes the techniques developed in the late 1950s by American poets such as Frank O'Hara. As Alvarez's copious citation of cultural intertexts suggests, however, a sense of historical belatedness is itself one of the distinguishing marks of postmodernism.

IV. The Twilight of the Avant-Garde: Spanish Poetry in the 1980s

Perhaps the single most significant development in Spanish poetry of the 1980s is a waning of the avant-garde impulse that has animated modern poetry from the early years of the twentieth century. One anthologist characterizes the poetry of the decade as "una poesía 'moderna' que por primera vez en este siglo, no se identifica con vanguardia"[30] ["A 'modern' poetry that for the first time in this century is not identified with the avant-garde"]. One symptom of the times is a changed attitude toward the literary and artistic past. The founding gesture of the avant-garde is a break with tradition. The modern artist makes use of cultural monuments by rewriting them, wrenching them from their original contexts: Duchamp paints a moustache on the Mona Lisa and provides an obscene caption. A similar attitude is evident in the last self-proclaimed avant-garde in Spanish letters, the novísimos of the late 1960s and 1970s. Questioning the artistic stultification of the immediate postwar period, these writers revindicate the poetic modernity of the prewar period. Despite the considerable distance between the postmodernism of the 1970s and the modernism of earlier decades, the novísimos still view themselves as a new manifestation of the avant-garde tradition of twentieth-century art.

The "culturalism" of the *novísimos* is often manifested in the form of a collage of intertextual references. A few of these poets work to invert traditional cultural hierarchies, privileging the detritus of culture over the canonical texts of Occidental literature: the poetry of Leopoldo María Panero comes to mind. Most of the *novísimos*, however, maintain a much more conservative (or conservationist) attitude toward the tradition. The poets who began to publish in the late 1970s and early 1980s have continued the more conservative tendency manifest in the work of poets such as Antonio Colinas. In contrast to the aggressive critique of culture undertaken by some of the *novísimos*, these younger writers often accept without question the value of traditionally prestigious works of art and literature.

In the work of Spanish poets of the 1980s, the citation of cultural intertexts often functions as an appropriation of aesthetic prestige from previously-consumed conventions and artifacts. In this section I propose to analyze this process of re-appropriation as a form of kitsch. This will entail a slight shift in the application of the term, which is often simply synonymous with bad taste or mass art: "To call something kitsch is in most cases a way of rejecting it outright as distasteful, repugnant, or even disgusting."[31] My definition, derived from Umberto Eco, emphasizes the dilution or trivialization of "high art" rather than the ugliness of the object. According to Eco, kitsch involves the prefabrication of self-consciously "artistic" effects. In this respect it refers more to the consumption than to the production of art works, since masterpieces are often the works that lend themselves most easily to trivialization:

> To love the Mona Lisa because it represents Mystery, or Ambiguity, or Ineffable Grace, or the Eternal Feminine, or because it is a more or less "sophisticated" topic of conversation ("Was it really a woman?" "Just think: one more brush stroke and that smile would have been different") means to accept a particular message not for itself but because of a previous decoding which, having now stiffened into a formula, sticks to the message like a tag.[32]

Although kitsch generally connotes popular consumption in addition to aesthetic dilution, not all mass culture shares kitsch's highbrow pretensions. Inversely, although kitsch often reaches a large audience, it is not necessarily an art for the masses. The vicarious aesthetic of kitsch can also underlie works that appeal primarily to a cultural elite. Among recent Spanish poets, in fact, the vicarious and private nature of aesthetic experience often corresponds to an indifference to the marketplace. Their work is rarely aesthetically jarring, and thus does not resemble the tacky mass-produced decorative objects commonly labelled as *kitsch*. Nevertheless, this poetry acquires its specifically "literary" quality at second hand, deriving its aesthetic validity from canonical aesthetic traditions of the past.

The younger Spanish poets' cannibalization of the literary tradition and their continued reliance on the *topoi* of the postromantic lyric considerably reduce the range and scope of their poetry. The dilution of the avant-garde impulse in Spanish poetry leads to an extremely limited and conventional view of the possibilities of the genre. Critics have insisted on the diversity of aesthetic postures assumed by the younger poets of the 1980s. Somewhat illogically, eclecticism itself is taken to be a "generational" signpost.[33] Still, a relatively coherent picture does emerge from a reading of representative books and anthologies of the decade.[34] Following Summerhill, I find a "surprisingly high degree of similarity" among younger Spanish poets.[35] Although generalizations are risky, it is difficult to discern the tremendous variety of aesthetic postures that these anthologists have touted. In contrast to the *novísimos*, who experiment with the limits of lyric poetry, the best-known poets of the 1980s remain content with an essentially conservative view of the genre. In addition to the vicarious aesthetic shared by many young poets, the operative conventions in their poetry include: (1) a deliberately sentimental, melancholy tone, with frequent echoes of the poetry of Francisco Brines; (2) a fixation on adolescence; (3) a desire to preserve an eternal moment of lyric experience; (4) an emphasis on the fragility and belatedness of the lyric *yo*; and (5) a pastiche of the great landmarks of modern poetry.

Like the *novísimos* of the 1960s and 1970s, recent Spanish poets allude to both popular and elite culture, often juxtaposing the two. References to the privileged texts of Western civilization, however, are especially frequent in the new poets of the 1980s.

Even in their citation of less privileged traditions such as jazz or cinema, they tend to strike a reverential pose. In contrast to the openly critical stance of many of the *novísimos,* they appear more willing to take for granted the validity of established culture, whatever its provenance, and to subsume their own voices into an ongoing tradition.

The work of Juan Lamillar (Sevilla, 1957) demonstrates both the strengths and weaknesses of the vicarious poetics that is so prevalent among poets of his age-group. In a review of *Muro contra la muerte,* Felipe Benítez Reyes, himself anthologized in García Martín, Ballena, and Villena, reveals the basic assumptions that animate Lamillar's poetry:

> . . . los asuntos de su libro están en lo cotidiano, pero también están pasados, y muy bien pasados, por el filtro de la literatura, del arte, que pone a la cotidianidad, a la pequeña esfera que es la vida de cualquier individuo, las invisibles alas con las que en el texto poético se eleva a la altura necesaria para que no la veamos ni demasiado cerca ni demasiasdo perdida en los celajes brumosos de la abstracción.[36]

> . . . the topics of his book belong to everyday reality, but they have also been filtered, and well filtered, through literature and art, which add to the everyday, to the small sphere that constitutes any individual's life, the invisible wings that the poetic text uses to rise to the heights required for us to see it neither too closely nor too distantly, lost in the misty clouds of abstraction.

The life of the individual poet is a "pequeña esfera," insignificant in itself and unrelated to any outside forces. Art is a filter through which everyday life must pass in order to gain literary legitimization. As Calinescu notes, "kitsch lends itself to a definition in terms of a systematic attempt to fly from daily reality."[37]

In his praise of Lamillar, Benítez Reyes privileges aesthetic distance, the idea that literature should shield the reader from the harshness—or in this case the boredom—of life. This doctrine represents the polar opposite of the "poetry of experience" of the 1950s and 1960s. The reader's relation to the reality depicted in a literary text is inevitably vicarious, indirect. Nevertheless, poets of the fifties and sixties such as Jaime Gil de Biedma, Angel González, and José Angel Valente envision the poet's task to be one of intensifying the force of lived experience rather than straining it through an aesthetic filter. Significantly, Benítez Reyes also rejects

cerebral abstraction, "los celajes brumosos de la abstracción."
Lamillar's poetry, he implies, has none of the aggressive intellec-
tuality that can be seen in poets of previous generations.

The aesthetic "filter" in Lamillar's work often takes the form of
explicit allusions to other works of art and literature. "Amor en
claroscuro," from *Música oscura*, provides a good example of this
technique:

> Cuando el recuerdo nos lo exija
> escribiremos tal vez sobre esta tarde
> de soñada nieve y de versos de Rilke,
> de amor en claroscuro.
> Pondremos el jazz sobre el papel
> como una taza de jazmín humeante,
> de embriagadoras sombras enemigas.
> Habremos de escribir sobre estas horas,
> sobre esta misma llegada de la noche
> con su disfraz de maga.
> Tú estás volviendo al mundo
> (a tu mundo de sueños)
> y yo anoto con calma, con minucia,
> con avaricia casi,
> los arduos pormenores de este instante,
> de esta habitación que da al recuerdo,
> que da a la lluvia, que da a tu nombre
> siempre, y al olvido.[38]

> When memory obliges us
> we will write perhaps of this afternoon
> of dreamed-for snow and Rilke's verse,
> of love in chiaroscuro.
> We will put jazz on the paper
> like a cup of steaming jasmine,
> of intoxicating hostile shadows.
> We'll have to write about these hours
> about this very nightfall
> in its sorceress' mask.
> You are returning to the world
> (to your world of dreams)
> and I take note, calmly, meticulously,
> almost greedily,
> of the arduous details of this moment,
> of the room that leads to memory,
> that leads to the rain, that leads to your name
> always, and to forgetfulness.

Culturalist allusions do not overwhelm the poem, as so often occurs with the *novísimos*. Rather, the passing mention of Rilke near the beginning of the poem serves to legitimate the poet's discourse, to certify its lyrical character. Why Rilke? Perhaps because he is one of the last great poets in the European tradition who unapologetically celebrates the poet's orphic power. Since Rilke is simply the "poet" by antonomasia ("Rilke el poeta" ["Rilke the poet"] as Blanca Andreu puts it),[39] it does not much matter which of his works the speaker and his companion are reading. The allusion, like the mention of jazz, is generic. Another Lamillar poem, "Jazz en el alcázar," recycles this musical tradition, converting it into cultural kitsch. It begins, "Los amigos te dicen: jazz de los años veinte" ["Your friends say: jazz of the 1920s"] and concludes by evoking "cualquier tema de Ellington, / aplausos y la noche y los amigos"[40] ["Any tune by Ellington, / applause and the night and friends"]. Again, the speaker does not care which of Duke Ellington's thousands of compositions he is hearing, or that Ellington's music is more characteristic of the 1930s and 1940s than of the 1920s. The cultural reference remains deliberately unspecified.

Despite its essentially second-hand aesthetics, Lamillar's poetry is elegant and even subtle in its deployment of lyric conventions. As García Martín comments, Lamillar's work strikes "un grato tono menor" ["a pleasing minor tone"].[41] In "Amor en claroscuro" the motif of the awakening woman calls to mind poems by Pedro Salinas and Claudio Rodríguez. Stylistically, the poem shows a mastery of rhetorical effects: note the adjective-noun-adjective combination ("embriagadoras sombras enemigas") and the climactic anaphora, modulated by enjambment, with which it concludes. The genuine subtlety of this poem, however, results from its play with temporal perspective. Writing from the present, the poet, like don Quijote leaving on his first sally, imagines the literary re-creation that will occur, "cuando el recuerdo nos lo exija" [when memory obliges us]. This retrospective glance, however, is anticipated in the poem at hand, which has prematurely converted the timeless lyric moment into a memory. This poet thus illustrates Lamillar's view of poetry as a way of living twice, once in life and a second time in its poetic simulacrum:

Concibo la poesía como una manera de rescatar el instante, de construir otra realidad. El tiempo detenido gracias a unas palabras con intensidad y tensión distintas a las del lenguaje común, gracias a un mundo personal creado con algunos temas obsesivos, con imágenes y ritmos. La poesía, pues, como un medio de *vivir dos veces*.[42]

I see poetry as a way of rescuing the moment, of constructing another reality. Time held still thanks to a few words that have an intensity and a tension distinct from those of common language, thanks to a personal world created out of some obsessive themes, out of images and rhythms. Poetry, then, as a way of *living twice*.

This conception of lyric poetry is utterly unremarkable. The practice of including such *poéticas* in anthologies implies that each poet will possess an original approach to his or her art. (The custom began with Gerardo Diego's landmark 1932 anthology.) Juan Lamillar, with all of his talent for language, is content to summarize the basic conventions of the postromantic lyric: the poet preserves a private world, stopping time through the creation of a more intense, poetic language different from that of ordinary speech.

One mark that distinguishes the "culturalism" of the younger poets from that of the *novísimos* is the diminished density and frequency of their citations. Their literary and artistic allusions appear less exaggerated and thus less vulnerable to parody. Some view the ebb of "Venetian" culturalism as a positive development. García Martín, for example, notes that Amalia Iglesias "rehúye las gratuitas referencias culturales" ["shies away from gratuitous cultural allusions"].[43] With this apparent gain in subtlety, however, the younger poets often sacrifice the force that comes from specificity. The result is a generic allusiveness that preserves the traditions of Western lyric poetry, but in a flattened form. It could be argued that the ostentatious erudition of the *novísimos*, in spite of its seeming gratuitousness, offers more intellectual and aesthetic substance.[44]

Juan Manuel Bonet (Paris, 1953) exemplifies the poetry of exhaustion that is so widespread among his contemporaries:

TODO ESTÁ ESCRITO

Otro poema que no dice sino
la sensación de estar solo,

tras un muro de viejos libros, viendo
cómo otro poeta dijo lo mismo
que lo escrito esta tarde,
sobre un tiempo que creíamos
únicamente nuestro, y tan presente.[45]

EVERYTHING IS WRITTEN

Another poem that says nothing except
the sensation of being alone,
behind a wall of old books, seeing
how another poet said the same thing
as this afternoon's writing,
about a time that we thought
was only ours, and so present.

The *topos* that this lyric reworks is, appropriately enough, the impossibility of novelty: there is nothing new under the sun. Guillermo Carnero's *Variaciones y figuras sobre un tema de La Bruyère,* one of the most significant books of the 1970s, is the most immediate precursor text. La Bruyère's theme, "Tout est dit et l'on vient trop tard" ["Everything is said and one comes too late"], provides Carnero with the occasion for a linguistically self-conscious examination of the limits of poetic language. Bonet, in contrast, prefers to evoke a particular mood rather than to explore issues in the philosophy of language.

Like Lamillar's "Amor en claroscuro," "Todo está escrito" superimposes another time frame onto the lyric present. Lamillar's poem emphasizes the uniqueness of the moment: "y yo anoto con calma, con minucia, / con avaricia casi, / los arduos pormenores de este instante." His desire to live his experience twice over leads him to create a poetic simulacrum, a verbal object validated by the poetic tradition. In Bonet's poem the repetition implicit in the conventions of the lyric genre annuls the originality of the poet's experience. As he begins to write, he realizes that the dead hand of tradition has already robbed him of the privileged moment that he would have liked to capture.

An obsession with cultural memory also characterizes the ostensibly "epic" poetry practiced by young writers such as Julio

Martínez Mesanza (Madrid, 1955). This poem from *Europa* resembles the more purely "lyric" poetry of Bonet:

RETIRADA

Vagan grises caballos por la senda
nevada, y un anciano se detiene
y ve pasar jinetes y armas oye.
Continuamente pasan los soldados,
y otra tierra recuerda y otro tiempo.
El corazón del viejo se ensombrece
mientras las muchas sombras enumera,
y otra guerra recuerda y otros hombres.[46]

RETREAT

Gray horses wander through the snowy
path, and an ancient man stops
and sees horseman pass and hears weapons.
The soldiers pass continuously
and he remembers another land in another time.
The old man's heart grows dark
as he counts the many shadows
and remembers another war and other men.

"Retirada" evokes a generally epic scene, one that could have occurred in any past century and in any part of Europe. As in "Todo está escrito," the present of the poem is reduced to a repetition of the past. The old man superimposes his memory of another retreat onto the one he is witnessing, but neither has any real specificity. Although the poem depicts a narrative scene rather than a solitary lyric speaker in the present, its effect is close to that of the more purely lyric poems of Bonet and Lamillar. Its vague evocation of a stereotypically epic event offers little historical or intellectual interest.

In spite of the "nueva épica," then, most Spanish poets of the 1980s have done little to question the limits of the lyric genre. The statements written for García Martín's anthology reiterate a traditional definition of lyric poetry. Andrés Trapiello's (León, 1953) is typical: "Tengo la impresión de que el poeta, mediante la poesía, parece que persigue quedar en el tiempo, permanecer, durar" ["I have the impression that the poet, through poetry, seems to seek to remain in time, to last, to endure"].[47] His self-definition is equally anachronistic: "A veces creo que mi actuali-dad es de no ser actual, como uno de esos oscuros personajes que en los *lieder* de Schubert, lamentándose del mundo, de sí mismos se lamentan, errabundos y a la merced de la vida" ["At times I believe that my currentness consists of not being current, like one of those dark characters from Schubert's *Lieder* who, la-menting reality, lament themselves, wandering and at the mercy of life"].[48] In the context of contemporary American poetry, Mar-jorie Perloff has argued that the postromantic lyric of individual subjectivity has become a minor genre: postmodern poets are now exploring other, nonlyric modes of poetry. She mentions the return of narrative forms in Frank O'Hara and Ed Dorn, the resurgence of prose poetry, David Antin's improvised "talk poems," and the chance-generated texts of John Cage and Jackson Mac Low. From this perspective, the minorness of recent Spanish poets, like that of many contemporary American poets, appears to be voluntary. It results from a deliberately limited set of options that belies any claim to a more inclusive postmodern eclecticism. Many talented and literate writers continue to practice a self-consciously nostalgic poetics, deriving their aesthetic credentials from a previously accepted lyric tradition. In contrast to the gen-eral drift in postmodern literature, they insist on the primacy of the subjective self in its relation to a privileged lyric experience.

The eclipse of the avant-garde impulse has led to a change in the relation of young poets to their modernist precursors. Even the strongest voices of the decade have not been able to escape a sense of belatedness with respect to the great modernist masters. In a poem dedicated to Lorca, Luis García Montero echoes Cer-nuda's "A Larra, con unas violetas" ["To Larra, with violets"] with the title "A Federico, con unas violetas." He concludes with a pastiche of Cernuda's famous poem: "Hoy no puede pesar sobre esta sombra / un ramo de violetas" ["Today a bouquet of violets / cannot weigh on this shadow"].[49] García Montero's gesture, of course, is deliberate, and the citation of such intertexts can, in theory, be a subtle and effective technique. In general terms, how-ever, Spanish poets of the 1980s tend to be "weak readers" of the tradition of modern poetry, from its romantic and symbolist founders to twentieth-century masters such as Rilke and Pound,

Jiménez, Cernuda and García Lorca. The title of Jon Jauristi's recent *Diario de un poeta recién cansado* (with its play on Juan Ramon
Jimenez's landmark *Diario de un poeta reciencasado*) expresses the
mood of fatigue with which younger poets approach the work of
their precursors.[50] Modernist poets have become classics to study,
revere, echo, pastiche, or parody. They are no longer live pres-
ences to be contested on equal ground.

Postmodernism has several contradictory meanings in contemporary culture. Its champions view it as a break with the conservatism implicit in modernist ideas of order (or, alternatively, as a
continuation of the avant-garde spirit of rebellion). In contrast,
critics of postmodernism writing from a left-wing perspective
have viewed it as a form of pastiche (or kitsch): "In a world in
which stylistic innovation is no longer possible, all that is left is
to imitate dead styles, to speak through the masks and with the
voices of an imaginary museum."[51] Whereas the work of José
Angel Valente and many of the *novísimos* could be said to be
postmodernist in the first sense, the poets of the 1980s have indeed tended to "imitate dead styles." In Spanish literary culture
the term *postmodernism* has already lost a greater part of its avant-
garde connotations. It has instead come to connote a vague air
of contemporaneity, without any specific intellectual or aesthetic
content. This dilution of the term explains how Barella is able to
label the poets in her anthology "postmodernists," even as she
emphasizes their conventionality.

In spite of their respect and admiration for their modernist and
postmodernist precursors, then, Spanish poets of the 1980s have
broken with the spirit that animates modern poetry from the
historic avant-garde of the early decades of the century through
the *novísimos*. They are literate and self-aware writers, but they
have felt no need to call into question the nature of language, the
role of the poet, or the frontiers of the lyric genre. The 1980s thus
represent a waning of the intellectually rigorous self-consciousness that has defined some of the most significant Spanish poetry
of the twentieth century.

Afterword

A predominant tendency among critics of Spanish poetry is to stress the general characteristics that link poets of the same period, generation, or school. Significant differences among writers, according to many accounts, result only from chronological development and historical change. This book, in contrast, has delineated some striking divergences between exact contemporaries as well as between poets of different periods: Salinas differs from Guillén, Valente from Gil de Biedma, Carnero from Alvarez. This emphasis on difference as opposed to similarity is partly a response to the present state of the field: the principal currents of twentieth-century Spanish poetry are well-established in the critical tradition, but the desire to group poets into generations, periods, and tendencies has, in my view, led to some overgeneralizations.

The writing of literary history is an arbitrary and contingent process by its very nature, and broad historical categories often fail to reflect a genuinely critical understanding of important poetic texts. In some cases, I would contend, revisionist readings of one or two key figures might be sufficient to force a reevaluation of previously accepted notions about the poetry of an entire period. Jorge Guillén, for example, is often taken as the paradigmatic poet of his time; yet other poets with whom he is commonly linked do not share his belief in the perfect fit between language and reality. José Angel Valente is also a poet who seems to define the ethos of a particular moment: his pronouncements on poetic language are often cited as representative of a broader generational poetics. His sacralization of the word, however, is at odds with Jaime Gil de Biedma's more matter-of-fact attitude toward the linguistic medium. It is difficult to decide which of these two influential poets is more typical of his time.

Although I have not undertaken a chronological survey in this book, my method does imply a particular vision of literary evolution. On the one hand, my critique of what I perceive to be over-simplifications hinders me from arriving at a schematic view of the historical development of Spanish poetry in this century. On the other hand there is another way to formulate the common elements among poets of the same time frame: literary moments can be defined in terms of dominant theoretical issues. Poets who do not share either a common style or a common attitude toward language might still share a common understanding of what these issues are, arriving at different solutions to a similarly defined set of problems.

This book has offered readings of poets of three distinct moments. Literary modernism, exemplified here by Salinas, Guillén, and Aleixandre, reflects a concern with linguistic representation. In these poets, the mirror becomes the central metaphor for language and its capacity, or incapacity, to reflect reality. Subsequent poets have not lost interest in the question of mimesis: it is fundamental to an understanding of both Valente and Carnero, for example. In recent years, however, emphasis has shifted onto other aspects of poetic language. I have not dealt in this book with Spanish poetry of the immediate postwar years, largely because the salient theoretical problem during this period took the form of a rather crude dichotomy between aestheticist dehumanization and social commitment. My own view is that the lack of a more nuanced vision of language contributed to a temporary impoverishment of poetic discourse, despite the vitality of gifted poets such as Blas de Otero.

The theoretical problems that most preoccupy midcentury poets like Valente, Gamoneda, and Gil de Biedma concern the legitimacy and authority of poetic discourse, its status among other discourses, and its philosophical foundations. As the direct successors to the social poets, they cannot ignore the problem of the poet's social role. The modernist concern with representation persists in the work of these writers, but it is reframed in ethical and at times in explicitly political terms. At stake is the capacity of poetic language, not just to reflect reality, but to intervene in the world. The clearest example of this attitude is Antonio Gamoneda's need to justify his paradoxical abandonment of the truth in *Descripción de la mentira*. His role as a poet is to bear witness to his solidarity with the oppressed, but he assumes this charge with a full consciousness of language's duplicity.

In the final period studied here, represented by the *novísimos* and their immediate successors, the dominant problem becomes the status of the poetic tradition itself, as younger poets situate their own work in reference to established conceptions of literariness.[1] These poets continue to be concerned with the legitimacy of poetic discourse, but they pose this question in more exclusively literary terms. In their focus on more narrowly poetic issues, younger Spanish poets reveal a greater kinship with the modernists than with the midcentury group. At the same time, their sense of literary history is quite distinct: where the modernists saw themselves as innovators, postmodern Spanish poets tend to be neotraditionalists, recycling the conventions they have inherited from the past.

Poetic self-consciousness, according to the hypothesis that I have proposed, will assume a new shape with each shift of the dominant theoretical paradigm. There are often notable similarities between two poets working within different paradigms: Salinas and Valente, for example, both propose a purification of poetic language. The change in cultural context, however, makes Valente's earnest and frustrated search for a sacralized *logos* very different from Salinas's more playful antimimeticism. The two poets give parallel answers to questions that are ultimately very distinct.

Although linguistic self-consciousness is not the exclusive property of any particular cohort of poets, it does seem to be the dominant poetic mode of the last thirty years (1960–1990). The later work of Vicente Aleixandre coincides with the early development of Claudio Rodríguez, Jaime Gil de Biedma, and José Angel Valente during the late 1950s and 1960s. Another group of poets, the *novísimos*, practice an overt form of metapoetry beginning in the late 1960s. Critics have recognized self-consciousness more readily among these poets than in the work of older generations, perhaps because of their obsessive use of "culturalist" intertextuality. It would be a mistake, however, to privilege this form of literary self-consciousness over other, equally rewarding, alternatives. The 1980s, finally, have seen important poetic statements by Valente and Antonio Gamoneda, a previously marginalized poet, and the emergence of the self-consciously literary voices of younger poets like Blanca Andreu and Juan Lamillar.

The single characteristic shared by all of the poets in this book is a preoccupation with poetic language. Shifting notions of the function and value of the word, however, make it impossible to define poetic language as an immutable essence: the image of language reflected in self-reflexive literature has taken a number of different forms in the past seventy years. Twentieth-century poetry is particularly rich in its capacity to rethink its basic definitions of both language and literature. The poetic self-consciousness that shapes the work of the most significant Spanish poets of this period evolves through time, reflecting fundamental changes in the status of poetry's linguistic medium.

Notes

Introduction

1. Andrew P. Debicki, *Poetry of Discovery: The Spanish Generation of 1956–71* (Lexington: University Press of Kentucky, 1982); Margaret Persin, *Recent Spanish Poetry and the Role of the Reader* (Lewisburg, Pa.: Bucknell University Press, 1987); C. Christopher Soufas, *Conflict of Light and Wind: The Spanish Generation of 1927 and the Ideology of Poetic Form* (Middletown, Conn.: Wesleyan University Press, 1989).

2. Philip Silver, *La casa de Anteo: Estudios de poética española (de Antonio Machado a Claudio Rodríguez* (Madrid: Taurus, 1985).

3. For a further elaboration of this approach to poetic language, see my *Claudio Rodríguez and the Language of Poetic Vision* (Lewisburg, Pa.: Bucknell University Press, 1990), 15–24.

4. I employ the term *modernism* to refer to the literary and artistic ferment of the first decades after World War I. In this context no reference to Spanish or Spanish-American *modernismo* is intended.

5. Linda Hutcheon, *The Poetics of Postmodernism: History, Theory, Fiction* (New York: Routledge, 1988); Marjorie Perloff, *The Poetics of Indeterminacy: Rimbaud to Cage* (Princeton: Princeton University Press, 1981). Perloff does not present her book as a theory of postmodernism per se, since indeterminacy is present in the "other tradition" of modernism as well. A good selection of essays on postmodernism in various contexts is *Zeitgeist in Babel: The Postmodernist Controversy*, ed. Ingeborg Hoesterev (Bloomington: Indiana University Press, 1991).

Chapter 1. Jorge Guillén and the Insufficiency of Poetic Language

1. Jorge Guillén, *Lenguaje y poesía: Algunos casos españoles* (Madrid: Revista de Occidente, 1962), 185; translated as *Language and Poetry* (Cambridge: Harvard University Press, 1961), 159. Subsequent references to *Lenguaje y poesía* will be incorporated into the text. The page number of the Spanish text will be given first, followed by that of the translation. All translations of other Spanish texts are my own, unless otherwise noted.

2. Howard Young, "Jorge Guillén and the Language of Poetry," *Hispania* 46 (March 1963): 66–77.

3. Debicki's view is fairly typical: "Al examinar detenidamente muchos poemas de Guillén—sean de *Cántico*, de *Clamor* o de *Homenaje*—encontraremos que todos ellos revelan simultáneamente un gran sentido do lo concreto y do lo inmediato, y la presencia de visiones más absolutas y universales" ["When we examine with care many of Guillén's poems—whether from *Cántico*, from *Clamor*

or from *Homenaje*—we find that all of them reveal simultaneously a great sense of the concrete and of the immediate, and the presence of more absolute and universal visions"]. Andrew P. Debicki, *La poesía de Jorge Guillén* (Madrid: Gredos: 1973), 20.

4. Gérard Genette, "Valéry and the Poetics of Language," in *Textual Strategies*, ed. Josué Harari (Ithaca: Cornell University Press, 1979), 359–73.

5. Ibid., 364. In the French version of this essay the equivalent sentence reads: "Compenser, mais aussi récompenser, puisque le défaut des langues est la raison d'être du 'vers,' qui n'existe que pour—et *de*—cette fonction compensatoire." *Mimologiques: Voyage en Cratylie* (Paris: Editions de Seuil, 1976), 274; original emphasis. For a more extended account of Mallarmé's poetics, see pages 257–78.

Guillén does not frame his argument in explicitly semiotic terms. Nor does he define exactly what it means for language to be sufficient in its representation of the world. In technical terms, one would have to distinguish the question of the motivation of the sign from that of *referentiality*, that is, the relation between language and reality. Guillén seems to be concerned primarily with the latter: he does not examine the nature of the linguistic sign itself. When I refer to "cratylism," therefore, I am extending the term to apply to both mimesis (in the linguistic sense) and referentiality. In Benveniste's view, Saussure himself confuses signified and referent in his original formulation of the arbitrariness of the sign: "It is clear that the argument is falsified by an unconscious and surreptitious recourse to a third term that was not included in the initial definition. This third thing is reality, the thing itself." Emile Benveniste, *Problems in General Linguistics*, trans. Mary Elizabeth Meek (Coral Gables, Fla.: University of Miami Press, 1971), 44.

6. Gustavo Adolfo Bécquer, *Rimas*, ed. José Luis Cano (Madrid: Cátedra, 1988), 45.

7. José Angel Valente, *Las palabras de la tribu* (Madrid: Siglo XXI, 1971), 66.

8. It is probable that Valente is responding directly to Guillén's opposition between sufficient and insufficient language. Significantly, the quotation from Dante's *Paradiso* that occasions Valente's title—"O quanto è corto il dire e come fioco / al mio concetto!"—is also cited in Guillén's discussion of San Juan de la Cruz (*Lenguaje y poesía*, 140).

9. Valente, *Las palabras de la tribu*, 116. The phrase *claroscuros* is taken directly from Guillén's *El argumento de la obra*. (Barcelona: Llibres de la Sinera, 1969), 71–81.

10. Robert Havard, *Jorge Guillén: Cántico* (London: Grant and Cutler, 1986), 118–19.

11. José Manuel Polo de Bernabé, *Conciencia y lenguaje en la obra de Jorge Guillén* (Madrid. Alfar, 1977) is a significant exception to this trend. Amparo Amorós considers Guillén's work as a reflection of the poetics of silence. Surprisingly, she does not attempt to reconcile this approach with more traditional views of the poet. "Palabra y silencio en la obra de Jorge Guillén," *Insula* 435–56 (February–March 1983): 4.

12. Jorge Guillén, *Cántico: fe de vida* (First Complete Edition. Buenos Aires: Sudamericana, 1950), 26.

13. Havard, 22.

14. José Manuel Blecua, "El poema 'Los nombres' de Jorge Guillén," *Insula* 435–56 (February–March 1983): 3.

15. There are several articles on Guillén's metapoetry, including Margaret Per-

sin, "The Metapoetic Text of Jorge Guillén," *Perspectives on Contemporary Literature* 8 (1982): 91–98; Martha Lafollette Miller, "Self-Commentary in Jorge Guillén's *Aire nuestro," Hispania* 65 (March 1982): 20–27. Both critics emphasize the way in which self-reflection reinforces rather than undercuts Guillén's faith in language.

16. Philip W. Silver, *La casa de Anteo: Estudios de poética hispánica (de Antonio Machado a Claudio Rodríguez.* (Madrid: Taurus, 1985), 135.

17. For Octavio Paz, Guillén is "the least intellectual poet of his generation, by which I do not mean that he is the least intelligent." *The Siren & the Seashell,* trans. Lysander Kemp and Margaret Sayers Peden. (Austin: University of Texas Press: 1976), 155–56.

18. Havard, 9.

19. Ibid., 9–11.

Chapter 2. Pedro Salinas and the Semiotics of Poetry

1. *Semiotics of Poetry* (Bloomington: Indiana University Press, 1978).

2. Ibid., 14.

3. Ibid., 19.

4. Jonathan Culler's clever critique of Riffaterre focuses on the incompatibility of textual and reader-response criticism: as an account of how readers actually make sense of texts, Riffaterre's theory cannot logically be in the position to produce such brilliantly novel readings. Riffaterre constantly contests other critics' interpretations of the texts he analyzes, implying that he is the first one to read them correctly. *The Pursuit of Signs* (Ithaca: Cornell University Press, 1981), 80–99. The basis of this complaint, I think, is the persistence of the mimetic impulse in reading, a tendency which contradicts Riffaterre's contention that the text obliges the reader to abandon mimesis.

5. Roland Barthes, *Essais Critiques* (Paris: Editions du Seuil, 1964), 106.

6. Ibid.

7. Pedro Salinas, *Poesías completas* (Barcelona: Barral, 1971), 107. Subsequent references to this collection will be incorporated into the text.

8. Pedro Salinas, *Lost Angel and Other Poems,* trans. Eleanor L. Trumbull (Baltimore: Johns Hopkins University Press, 1938), 119–21.

9. Stéphane Mallarmé, *Oeuvres complètes* (Paris: Gallimard, 1945), 38.

10. Luis de Góngora, *Sonetos completos,* ed. Biruté Ciplijauskaité (Madrid: Castalia, 1969), 138.

11. Although this poem is an extreme example, overt redundancy is frequent in Salinas's poems, which often explicitly take the form of theme and variations. Riffaterre himself notes the foregrounding of semiotic overdetermination in a prose poem by Francis Ponge. *Text Production* (New York: Columbia University Press, 1983), 261.

12. Julian Palley, *La luz no usada: la poesía de Pedro Salinas* (México: Andrea, 1966), 35–36.

13. Andrew P. Debicki, *Estudios sobre la poesía española contemporánea* (Madrid: Gredos, 1968), 71.

14. David Stixrude more aptly views Salinas's enemy here as "preordained formulas," *The Early Poetry of Pedro Salinas* (Madrid: Castalia, 1975), 85–87.

15. In a study of "Arena" and other early poems, Andrew Debicki notes the presence of mutually incompatible interpretations that force the reader into an

aporia. He also compares the self-referentiality of "Cuartilla" to that of another poem, "Underwood Girls." "The Play of Difference in the Early Poetry of Pedro Salinas," *MLN* 100 (March 1985): 265–80.

16. Salinas, *Lost Angel and Other Poems*, 148–49.

17. Philip W. Silver, *La casa de Anteo: Estudios de Poética Hispánica (De Antonio Machado a Claudio Rodríguez* (Madrid: Taurus, 1985), 118–47.

18. Ibid., 136.

19. Riffaterre explains: "The theoretical aims of this book make it applicable, I believe, to all Western literature, and in all likelihood some of the rules I propose reflect universals of literary language. But I have used only French examples, primarily from nineteenth- and twentieth-century writers (my specialization, aside from poetics.)" Riffaterre, *Semiotics of Poetry*, ix.

20. Ibid., 1.

21. Why not? Eco adduces several reasons. The "referent" of the image cannot be absent. Furthermore, it "is not independent of its medium or channel" and "cannot be interpreted." Umberto Eco, *Semiotics and the Philosophy of Language* (Bloomington: Indiana University Press, 1984), 216–17.

22. Ibid., 210.

23. Claudio Rodríguez, *Desde mis poemas* (Madrid: Cátedra, 1983), 40.

24. The feminist implications of Salinas's linguistic mirror should be obvious by this point. Not only is woman the object of the masculine gaze, but the poet assumes the role of an obsessive surgeon whose essentialization causes her tangible pain:

> Perdóname por ir así buscándote
> tan torpemente, dentro
> de ti.
> Perdóname el dolor, alguna vez.
> Es que quiero sacar
> de ti tu mejor tú.
>
> (*Poesías completas*, 285)

> Forgive me for searching for you like this
> so clumsily, within
> yourself.
> Forgive me the occasional pain.
> It's because I want to extract
> from you your best you.

25. Antonio Blanch, *La poesía pura española: Conexiones con la cultura francesa* (Madrid: Gredos, 1976); Juan Cano Ballesta, *La poesía española entre pureza y revolución (1930–1936)* (Madrid: Gredos, 1972).

Chapter 3. Vicente Aleixandre: "Límites y espejo"

1. Carlos Bousoño, *La poesía de Vicente Aleixandre*. 3rd ed. (Madrid: Gredos, 1977). The most complete treatment of Aleixandre's poetics is Dario Puccini, "Modalidades y desarrollos internos de la poética aleixandrina," *La palabra poética de Vicente Aleixandre* (Barcelona: Ariel, 1979), 148–91. See also Randolph Pope, "Vicente Aleixandre y las limitaciones del lenguaje," in *Vicente Aleixandre: A Critical Appraisal*, ed. Santiago Daydí-Tolson (Ypsilanti, Mich.: Bilingual Press, 1981), 245–57.

2. Philip Silver, *La casa de Anteo: Estudios de poética española (de Antonio Machado a Claudio Rodríguez* (Madrid: Taurus, 1985), pp. 148–156.

3. Vicente Aleixandre, *Obras completas* 2 vols. (Madrid: Aguilar, 1978), 2:645; emphasis in original. Subsequent references to this volume will be incorporated into the text.

4. As Puccini has aptly stated, the implied target of these remarks is probably Juan Ramón Jiménez (*La palabra poética de Vicente Aleixandre*, 157–60).

5. *Corriente alterna* (México: Siglo Veintiuno, 1967), 7.

6. Vicente Aleixandre, *Espadas como labios. La destrucción o el amor*, ed. José Luis Cano (Madrid: Castalia, 1972), 85. I cite this edition instead of the *Obras completas*, since the editor reproduces the absence of punctuation found in the original 1932 edition of the book. Other critics have recognized the metapoetic dimension of *Espadas como labios:* "Puede afirmarse sin ambages que se trata de una *poesía del lenguaje* en sus relaciones con el pensamiento que a veces llega a la temática del metalenguaje" ["We can plainly affirm that it is a *poetry of language* in relation to thought that at times reaches the thematics of metalanguage"]. (Yolanda Novo Villaverde, *"Pasión de la tierra* y *Espadas como labios:* Aspectos cosmovisionarios y simbología surrealistas," in Daydí-Tolson, 122–44, 125). "La cosmovisión aleixandrina—sin discusión, al menos, la del 'primer Aleixandre'— se sustenta, trabadamente, indisolublemente, en el lenguaje. Ya que su universo, por ser de ideas o de sensaciones, no es espejo de realidad sea cual sea la deformación o floritura del vidrio, sino espejo de lenguaje" ["Aleixandre's poetic vision—at least, without any argument, that of the 'first Aleixandre,' is based, indissolubly, on language. For his universe, consisting of ideas or sensations, is not a mirror of reality, with whatever deformation or decoration of the glass, but a mirror of language"]. Luis Antonio de Villena, "La luna, astro final del "Primer Aleixandre" (Algo sobre *Mundo a solas*)," *Insula* 368–69 (July–August 1977): 8, 33.

7. Paul Illie, "Descent and Castration," Daydi-Tolson, 104–21.

8. Aleixandre, *Espadas como labios*, 45.

9. Roman Jakobson, "Closing Statement: Linguistics and Poetics," in *Semiotics: An Introductory Anthology*, ed. Robert E. Innis (Bloomington: Indiana University Press, 1985), 147–75.

10. Sylvia Sherno has studied a similar paradox in her discussion of Blas de Otero's *Esto no es un libro*, a book whose title comes from *Leaves of Grass*. "The Paradox of Poetry in Blas de Otero's *Esto no es un libro*," *Hispania* 70: 40 (December, 1987): 768–75.

11. Myriam Najt's article on this poem is too narrow in scope to fulfill the promise of its title: "La palabra 'palabra' en 'Las palabras del poeta'" *Cuadernos Hispanoamericanos* 352–54 (October–December 1979): 581–93.

12. Pere Gimferrer, "La poesía última de Vicente Aleixandre," in *Vicente Aleixandre*, ed. José Luis Cano (Madrid: Taurus, 1977), 265–73.

13. Guillermo Carnero distinguishes two modes of knowledge: *conocer* is a direct and vital discovery of reality in all of its immediacy, whereas *saber* is the lucidity that results from the loss of this immediacy. Carnero identifies language with *saber*, and views it in negative terms as an essentially sterile mode of representation. "'Conocer' y 'saber' en *Poemas de la consumación* y *Diálogos del conocimiento*," Cano, *Vicente Aleixandre*, 274–82.

14. Aleixandre anticipates many of the preoccupations of *Poemas de la consu-*

mación in a set of poems grouped under the rubric "Nacimiento último" [Final birth] (*Obras completas,* 1:609–24).

Chapter 4. The Word Made Flesh: Logocentrism in the Later Work of José Angel Valente

1. See Andrew P. Debicki, *Poetry of Discovery: The Spanish Generation of 1956–71* (Lexington: University of Kentucky Press, 1982), 1–19. This book includes studies of Francisco Brines, Claudio Rodríguez, Angel González, Gloria Fuertes, José Angel Valente, Jaime Gil de Biedma, Carlos Sahagún, Eladio Cabañero Angel Crespo, and Manuel Mantero. My use of *generation* and roughly equivalent terms is not meant to promote a generational theory of literary evolution. The only advantage of maintaining some notion of a group is to be able to participate in the ongoing critical discussion of these poets: it is often productive to compare the work of poets whose lives and careers correspond chronologically.

2. Valente's poetry through 1980 is collected in *Punto Cero: Poesía 1953–1979* (Barcelona: Barral, 1980). He has published four major books of poetry in the 1980s: *Tres lecciones de tinieblas* (Barcelona: La Gaya Ciencia, 1980); *Mandorla* (Madrid: Cátedra, 1982); *El fulgor* (Madrid: Cátedra, 1984); and *Al dios del lugar* (Barcelona: Tusquets, 1989). His essays are collected in *Las palabras de la tribu* (Barcelona: Siglo XXI, 1971) and *La piedra y el centro* (Madrid: Taurus, 1982). Subsequent references to Valente's publications will be incorporated into the main body of the text.

3. Andrew P. Debicki, "Una poesía de la postmodernidad: los novísimos," *Anales de la Literatura Española Contemporánea* 14 (1989): 33–50.

4 Ibid., 35.

5. See, for example, Martha LaFollette Miller, "Claudio Rodríguez's Linguistic Skepticism: A Counterpart to Jorge Guillén's Linguistic Faith," *Anales de la Literatura Española Contemporánea* 6 (1981): 105–21.

6. This is Debicki's basic approach in his chapter "José Angel Valente: Reading and Rereading," *Poetry of Discovery,* 102–22. Useful commentaries on Valente's metapoetry include José Olivio Jiménez, "Lucha, duda y fe en la palabra poética: A través de *La memoria y los signos* de José Angel Valente," *Diez años de poesía española: 1960–1970* (Madrid: Insula, 1972), 223–42; Margaret H. Persin, "Theories of Language in Valente's 'Poemas a Lázaro,'" *Recent Spanish Poetry and the Role of the Reader* (Lewisburg, Pa.: Bucknell University Press, 1987), 26–44; and Anita Hart, "The Poet in José Angel Valente's Metapoetic Texts," *Hispanic Journal* 11, 2 (Fall 1990): 123. I approach Valente's metapoetry through the perspective of gender in "El signo de la feminidad': Gender and Poetic creation in José Angel Valente," *Revista de Estudios Hispánicos* 25, 2 (May 1991): 123–33.

Books exclusively devoted to Valente's work include Ellen Engelson Marson, *Poesía y poética de José Angel Valente* (New York: Eliseo Torres and Sons, 1978); Santiago Daydí-Tolson, *Las voces y los ecos en la poesía de José Angel Valente* (Lincoln, Neb.: Society of Spanish and Spanish-American Studies, 1984); and Miguel Mas, *La escritura material de José Angel Valente* (Madrid: Hiperión, 1987), the only one of the three that treats the poetry of the 1980s at length. A useful bibliography of secondary sources is included in José Angel Valente, *Entrada en materia,* ed. Jacques Ancet (Madrid: Cátedra, 1985), 36–39.

7. Peter Dunn, "Don Juan Manuel: The World as Text," *MLN* 106 (March 1991): 227–28.

8. Anita Hart, "The Poet in José Angel Valente's Metapoetic Texts," 123.

9. Claudio Rodríguez, *Desde mis poemas* (Madrid: Cátegra, 1984), 252.

10. Jacques Derrida, *Of Grammatology,* trans. Gayatri Chakravorty Spivak (Baltimore: Johns Hopkins University Press, 1976).

11. See "José Lezama Lima," *Punto cero,* 360, and the untitled prose poem beginning "Maestro, usted dijo," *Mandorla,* 48.

12. Walter J. Ong, *Orality and Literacy: The Technologizing of the Word* (London and New York: Methuen, 1982), 74.

13. Ibid., 75.

14. Douglass Rogers contrasts the loss of faith in language among Spanish poets during the postwar period to the confident attitudes of older poets: "Posturas del poeta ante su palabra en la España de posguerra," in *After the War: Essays on Recent Spanish Poetry,* eds. Salvador Jiménez-Fajardo and John Wilcox (Boulder, Co.: Society of Spanish and Spanish-American Studies, 1988), pp. 55–65. The idea that postwar poets oppose "la deificación del verbo poético" (p. 63), nevertheless, must be qualified.

15. See Jonathan Mayhew, *Claudio Rodríguez and the Language of Poetic Vision* (Lewisburg, Pa.: Bucknell University Press, 1990), for a more complete discussion of Rodríguez's poetry and poetics.

16. This motif recurs frequently in *Poetry of Discovery,* applied to individual poets and to the generation as a whole: "seemingly direct language" (1), "seemingly ordinary language" (20), "seemingly everyday language" (40), "The language of Sahagún's verse seems ordinary." (142).

17. Ibid., 110.

18. Ibid., 17.

Chapter 5. Rhetoric and Truth in Antonio Gamoneda's *Descripción de la mentira*

1. See Santos Alonso, *Literatura leonesa actual* (Valladolid: Junta de Castilla y León, 1986): 205–207; Francisco Martínez García, *Historia de la literatura leonesa* (Madrid: Editorial Everest, 1982), 810–23; Miguel Casado, *Esto era y no era: Lectura de poetas de Castilla y León* vol. 1 (Valladolid: Ambito, 1985), 97–118. Casado's introduction to *Edad,* Gamoneda's collected poetry, is substantially similar to his essay in *Esto era y no era.*

2. Antonio Gamoneda, *Edad (Poesía 1947–1986),* ed. Miguel Casado (Madrid: Cátedra, 1988), 63. Subsequent references to this edition will be incorporated into the text.

3. Claudio Rodríguez, *Desde mis poemas* (Madrid: Cátedra, 1984), p. 129.

4. I have chosen the word *passage* to designate each of the smaller divisions of the poem, separated by larger spaces than the individual lines. At the risk of distorting the integrity of the text, I omit several lines from my analysis here for the sake of economy of presentation. The remainder of the first section is reproduced in its entirety.

5. Richard Rorty, *Contingency, Irony and Solidarity* (New York: Cambridge University Press, 1989), 61.

6. Ibid., 28.

7. Quoted in Pedro Provencio, *Poéticas españolas contemporáneas: La generación del 50* (Madrid: Hiperión, 1988), 71–72.

Chapter 6. Jaime Gil de Biedma's *Moralidades:* Rationalism and Poetic Form

1. José Angel Valente, *Las palabras de la tribu* (Barcelona: Siglo XXI de Editores, 1971), 7.

2. Andrew Debicki's chapter, "Gil de Biedma and the Theme of Illusion," *Poetry of Discovery: The Spanish Generation of 1956–71* (Lexington: Kentucky University Press, 1982), 121–41, explores the way Gil de Biedma's poetry transcends its only apparently realistic mode. Pere Rovira's book, *La poesía de Jaime Gil de Biedma* (Barcelona: Edicions de Mall, 1986) is a competent academic study, although the segregated treatment of *temas* and *estilo* is disappointing: one of the fascinating aspects of Gil de Biedma's work is precisely the intersection of theme and style. Carme Riera, in *La escuela de Barcelona: Barral, Gil de Biedma, Goytisolo: el núcleo poético de la generación de los 50* (Barcelona: Anagrama, 1988), studies the poet's work in its social and literary context.

3. "Por los caminos de la irracionalidad: notas sobre irrealismo e irracionalidad en la poesía de Jaime Gil de Biedma," *Insula* 523–24 (July–August 1990): 48–52.

4. Jaime Gil de Biedma, *El pie de la letra: Ensayos 1955–1979* (Barcelona: Editorial Critica, 1980), 56.

5. Ibid., 57.

6. Jaime Gil de Biedma, *Las personas del verbo* (Barcelona: Seix Barral, 1982), pp. 102, 143. Subsequent references to this volume, which includes all the poetry the author wished to preserve, will be incorporated into the text.

7. *El pie de la letra*, 17–31.

8. *In Defense of Reason* (New York: The Swallow Press and William Morrow and Company, 1947), 464.

9. Roland Barthes, *Le degré zéro de l'écriture* (Paris: Editions de Seuil, 1953).

10. Winters, *In Defense of Reason*, 464–46.

11. Robert Langbaum's *Poetry of Experience* (New York: Random House, 1957), a study of the dramatic monologue, influenced many Spanish poets of this period.

12. On the sestina as a generative device in the postmodern American poetry of Louis Zukovsky and John Ashbery, see Joseph M. Conte, *Unending Design: The Forms of Postmodern Poetry* (Ithaca: Cornell University Press, 1991), 167–92.

13. Angel González, *Palabra sobre palabra* (Barcelona: Seix Barral, 1986), 291–94.

14. Gloria Fuertes, *Obras incompletas* (Madrid: Cátedra, 1983), 141.

15. José Angel Valente, *Material memoria* (Barcelona: La Gaya ciencia, 1979), 63.

16. Claudio Rodríguez, *Desde mis poemas* (Madrid: Cátedra, 1984), 40.

Chapter 7. Postmodernism, Culturalism, Kitsch

1. José María Castellet, *Nueve nosísimos poetas españoles* (Barcelona: Barral, 1970). The nine poets originally included in Castellet's anthology are José María Alvarez, Manuel Vázquez Montalbán, Antonio Martínez Sarrión, Vicente Molina Foix, Ana María Moix, Félix de Azúa, Guillermo Carnero, Pedro Gimferrer, and

Leopoldo María Panero. Molina Foix and Moix have written little poetry since 1970, distinguishing themselves in prose fiction. Vázquez Montalbán has also become better known for his fiction than for his poetry.

2. Castellet, 108.

3. Guillermo Carnero, *Ensayo de una teoría de la visión: Poesía 1966–1977* (Madrid: Hiperión, 1979; 2nd ed. 1983), 181.

4. Luis Cernuda, *La realidad y el deseo* (Madrid: Ediciones F.C.E., 1970), 461.

5. Pere Gimferrer, *Poemas: 1962–1969* (Madrid: Visor, 1988), 104.

6. Carnero's must influential poetry of the 1960s and 1970s is collected in *Ensayo de una teoría de la visión: Poesía 1966–1977*. References to this volume, abbreviated as *Ensayo,* will be incorporated into the main body of the text. Carnero has published one additional collection, *Divisibilidad indefinida* (Sevilla: Renacimiento, 1990).

The three most extensive treatments of Carnero's work are: José Olivio Jiménez, "'Estética del lujo y de la muerte': Sobre *Dibujo de la muerte* (1967), de Guillermo Carnero," *Diez años de poesía española (1960–1970)* (Madrid: Insula, 1972), 375–85; Ignacio Javier López, "Metonimia y negación: *Variaciones y figuras sobre un tema de La Bruyère* de Guillermo Carnero," *Hispanic Review* 54 (Summer 1986): 257–77; and Carlos Bousoño's introduction to *Ensayo de una teoría de la visión,* "La poesía de Guillermo Carnero," 11–68.

7. José Olivio Jiménez convincingly argues that Carnero's early aestheticism is a death mask, thus defending the poet against the charge of sterile art-for-art's-sake.

8. Angel González, *Palabra sobre palabra* (Barcelona: Seix Barral, 1986), 310.

9. Mirta Camandone de Cohen, "Asedio a la poesía de Guillermo Carnero," *Hispanic Journal* 7 (Fall 1985): 123–29, 128.

10. "Fabrizio" is probably the prominent Danish entomologist Johann Christian Fabricius (1745–1808). The embryologist Hieronymus Fabricius of Aquapendente (1537–1619) is another possibility. I have not been able to find the source of Carnero's anecdote.

11. Paul Valéry, *Oeuvres* 2 vols. (Paris: Gallimard, 1960), 2:92.

12. Carnero himself notes that technical terms can acquire a poetic connotation: "toda terminología especializada adquiere, por su sentido arcano / y supuestamente preciso, un gran valor poético" [all specialized terminology acquires, through its arcane / and supposedly precise meaning, a great poetic value] (*Ensayo,* 157).

13. "La corte de los poetas: Los últimos veinte años de poesía española en castellano," *Revista de Occidente* 23 (April 1983): 43–59, 57.

14. José María Alvarez, *El escudo de Aquiles* (Madrid: Ediciones del dragón, 1987), 61.

15. Criticism on Alvarez's poetry is limited in quantity. See P. L. Ugalde, "José María Alvarez, o el arte de la cita," *Hora de Poesía* 3 (May–June 1979): 33–36; Xavier Seoane, "Sobre *Museo de cera,*" *Cuadernos Hispanoamericanos* 459 (September 1988): 69–78; Thomas R. Franz, Review of *Museo de cera, Hispania* 59 (March 1976): 174–75. *Al otro lado del espejo (Conversaciones con José María Alvarez),* ed. Csaba Csuday (Murcia: Universidad de Murcia, 1987), contains several "testimonios" of some critical interest, along with interviews that reveal Alvarez's literary personality.

16. Franz, 175.

17. José María Alvarez, *Museo de Cera* (Madrid: Hiperión, 1978), 157. Subsequent references to this volume will be incorporated into the text.

18. Franz, 175.

19. T. S. Eliot, *Selected Essays* (New York: Harcourt, Brace and Company, 1932), 5.

20. Clement Greenberg, "The Notion of 'Postmodern,'" in *Zeitgeist in Babel: The Postmodernist Controversy*, ed. Ingeborg Hoesterey (Bloomington: Indiana University Press, 1991), 45.

21. Ezra Pound has been a dominant influence on postmodern poets who wish to escape from the narrow bonds of lyric poetry. Both O'Hara and Alvarez create a tissue of cultural references, a technique ultimately derived from Pound's *Cantos*. The difference between the modern and the postmodern attitude toward these references, however, is quite notable. Pound used citations as documentary evidence that validated his historical vision. His faith in the referentiality of language, the capacity of a concrete image to evoke the reality of other historical epochs, contrasts with the linguistic skepticism inherent in the work of postmodern poets, who adopt Poundian techniques of free verse, cultural citation, and the series of apparently disconnected images while eliminating the specific ideological content of Pound's historical vision.

22. Charles Olson, *Additional Prose*, ed. George F. Butterick (Bolinas, Calif.: Four Seasons Foundation, 1974), 40. In spite of Olson's early use of the term, it did not gain wide currency until much later.

23. Donald M. Allen, ed., *The New American Poetry: 1945–1960* (New York: Grove Press, 1960).

24. For an alternative view see Jerome Mazzaro, *Postmodern American Poetry* (Urbana: University of Illinois Press, 1980). Mazzaro traces the genesis of postmodern poetry to W. H. Auden, and studies such figures as Randall Jarrell, Elizabeth Bishop, Theodore Roethke, and John Berryman. These poets represent an aesthetically conservative, "academic" tradition against which the poets included in Don Allen's anthology were reacting.

25. Frank O'Hara, *The Collected Poems of Frank O'Hara* (New York: Knopf, 1971), 341.

26. Alvarez, *El escudo de Aquiles*, 77.

27. O'Hara, 366.

28. Ibid., 335.

29. Linda Hutcheon, *The Poetics of Postmodernism: History, Theory, Fiction* (New York: Routledge, 1988).

30. Julia Barella, ed., *Después de la modernidad. Poesía española en sus lenguas literarias* (Barcelona: Anthropos, 1987), 14.

31. Matei Calinescu, *Faces of Modernity: Avant-garde, Decadence, Kitsch* (Bloomington: Indiana University Press, 1977), 235.

32. Umberto Eco, *The Open Work*, Anna Cangogni, trans. (Cambridge: Harvard University Press, 1989), 197.

33. Barella, 9; Luis Antonio de Villena, ed., *Postnovísimos* (Madrid: Visor, 1986), 18–20.

34. Stephen J. Summerhill notes the practical difficulties of studying very recent poetry: "Spanish Poetry of the Eighties: Some Problems of Definition," *España Contemporánea* 2, 4 (Spring 1989): 103. Following his lead, I have consulted Luis Antonio de Villena, ed., *Postnovísimos* (Madrid: Visor, 1986); Julia Barella, ed., *Después de la modernidad*, and García Martín, ed. *La generación de los ochenta* (Valencia: Poesía Valencia, 1988). Ramón Buenaventura, ed., *Las diosas blancas: Antología de la joven poesía española escrita por mujeres* 2nd ed. (Madrid: Hiperión, 1986) collects the work of numerous women poets of the 1980s. Although these

writers are not immune from the temptations of kitsch, their work raises other issues that are beyond the scope of my argument here.

35. Summerhill, 108.

36. Felipe Benítez Reyes, review of Lamillar, Juan, *Muro contra la muerte. Insula* 451 (1984): 10.

37. Calinescu, 244.

38. Juan Lamillar, *Música oscura* (Sevilla: Renacimiento, 1984), 50–51.

39. This phrase occurs as a leitmotif in Blanca Andreu, *De una niña de provincias que se vino a vivir en un Chagall* 5th ed. (Madrid: Hiperión, 1986), 13, 33, 37, etc. An ungenerous assessment of Andreu's work would view it as surrealist kitsch, a pastiche of Lorca and other writers. In contrast to many male writers of her generation, however, her voice is relatively strong and fresh.

40. Lamillar, 23.

41. García Martín, 38.

42. Ibid., p. 150; original emphasis.

43. Ibid., p. 13.

44. Villena, 23–25, also warns of the dangers of the excessive traditionalism of younger poets, but he does not name the guilty parties. The poets in his book tend to be more self-consciously "hip" and up-to-date than those in the other recent anthologies.

45. Juan Manuel Bonet, *La patria oscura* (Madrid: Trieste, 1983), 17.

46. García Martín, 143.

47. Ibid., 118.

48. Ibid., 199.

49. Ibid., 119.

50. Jon Jauristi, *Diario de un poeta recién cansado* (Pamplona: Pamiela, 1986).

51. Fredric Jameson, "Postmodernism and Consumer Society," Hal Foster, ed. *The Anti-Aesthetic* (Port Townsend, Wash.: Bay Press, 1983), 115.

Afterword

1. For a confirmation of this thesis, see Ignacio Javier López, "El silencio y la piedra: metáforas de la tradición en la poesía española contemporánea," *Bulletin of Hispanic Studies* 57 (January 1990): 43–56.

Bibliography

Aleixandre, Vicente. *Espadas como labios. La destrucción o el amor.* Edited by José Luis Cano. Madrid: Castalia, 1972.

———. *Obras completas.* 2 vols. Madrid: Aguilar, 1978.

Alonso, Santos. *Literatura leonesa actual.* Valladolid: Junta de Castilla y León, 1986.

Allen, Donald, M., ed. *The New American Poetry: 1945–1960.* New York: Grove Press, 1960.

Alvarez, José María. *El escudo de Aquiles.* Madrid: Ediciones del Dragón, 1987.

———. *Museo de cera (Manual de exploradores).* Madrid: Hiperión, 1978.

Amorós, Amparo. "Palabra y silencio en la obra de Jorge Guillén." *Insula* 435–36 (February–March 1983): 4.

Andreu, Blanca. *De una niña de provincias que se vino a vivir en un Chagall.* 5th ed. Madrid: Hiperión, 1986.

Barella, Julia, ed. *Después de la modernidad: Poesía española en sus lenguas literarias.* Barcelona: Anthropos, 1987.

Barthes, Roland. *Le degré zéro de l'écriture.* Paris: Editions de Seuil, 1953.

———. *Essais Critiques.* Paris: Editions du Seuil, 1964.

Bécquer, Gustavo Adolfo. *Rimas.* Edited by José Luis Cano. Madrid: Cátedra, 1988.

Benítez Reyes, Felipe. Review of Juan Lamillar, *Muro contra la muerte. Insula* 451 (1984): 10.

Benveniste, Emile. *Problems in General Linguistics.* Translated by Mary Elizabeth Meek. Coral Gables, Fla.: Miami University Press, 1971.

Blanch, Antonio. *La poesía pura española: Conexiones con la cultura francesa.* Madrid: Gredos, 1976.

Blecua, José Manuel. "El poema 'Los nombres' de Jorge Guillén." *Insula* 435–36 (February–March 1983): 3.

Bonet, Juan Manuel. *La patria oscura.* Madrid: Trieste, 1983.

Bousoño, Carlos. *La poesía de Vicente Aleixandre.* 3rd ed. Madrid: Gredos, 1977.

———. *Poesía poscontemporánea: cuatro estudios y una introducción.* Madrid: Júcar, 1984.

Buenaventura, Ramón, ed. *Las diosas blancas: Antología de la joven poesía escrita por mujeres.* 2nd ed. Madrid: Hiperión, 1986.

Calinescu, Matei. *Faces of Modernity: Avant-garde, Decadence, Kitsch.* Bloomington: Indiana University Press, 1977.

Camandone de Cohen, Mirta. "Asedio a la poesía de Guillermo Carnero." *Hispanic Journal* 7 (Fall 1985): 123–29.

Cano, José Luis, ed. *Vicente Aleixandre.* Madrid: Taurus, 1977.

Cano Ballesta, Juan. *La poesía española entre pureza y revolución (1930–1936).* Madrid: Gredos, 1972.

Carnero, Guillermo. "'Conocer' y 'saber' en *Poemas de la consumación y Diálogos del conocimiento.*" In Cano, ed. *Vicente Aleixandre,* 274–82.

———. "La corte de los poetas: Los últimos veinte años de poesía española en castellano." *Revista de occidente* 23 (April 1983): 43–59.

———. *Divisibilidad indefinida.* Sevilla: Renacimiento, 1990.

———. *Ensayo de una teoría de la visión.* Madrid: Hiperión, 1979; 2nd ed., 1983.

Casalduero, Joaquín. "La voz del poeta: Aire nuestro." Jorge Guillén. *Obra poética: antología.* Madrid: Alianza, 1970. 7–23.

Casado, Miguel. *Esto era y no era: Lectura de poetas de Castilla y León.* Vol. 1. Valladolid: Ambito, 1985.

Castellet, José María. *Nueve novísimos poetas españoles.* Barral: Barcelona, 1970.

Cernuda, Luis. *La realidad y el deseo.* Madrid: Ediciones F. C. E., 1970.

Conte, Joseph M. *Unending Design: The Forms of Postmodern Poetry.* Ithaca: Cornell University Press, 1991.

Culler, Jonathan. *The Pursuit of Signs.* Ithaca: Cornell University Press, 1981.

Daydí-Tolson, Santiago. *Las voces y los ecos en la poesía de José Angel Valente.* Lincoln, Ne.: Society of Spanish and Spanish-American Studies, 1984.

———, ed. *Vicente Aleixandre: A Critical Appraisal.* Ypsilanti, Mich.: Bilingual Press, 1981.

Debicki, Andrew P. *La poesía de Jorge Guillén.* Madrid: Gredos, 1973.

———. *Poetry of Discovery: The Spanish Generation of 1956–71.* Lexington: University of Kentucky Press, 1982.

———. "Una poesía de la postmodernidad: Los novísimos." *Anales de la Literatura Española Contemporánea* 14 (1989): 33–50.

Derrida, Jacques. *Of Grammatology.* Translated by Gayatri Spivak. Baltimore: Johns Hopkins University Press, 1976.

Dunn, Peter. "Don Juan Manuel: The World as Text." *MLN* 106 (March 1991): 227–28.

Eco, Umberto. *The Open Work.* Translated by Anna Cangogni. Cambridge: Harvard University Press, 1989.

———. *Semiotics and the Philosophy of Language.* Bloomington: Indiana University Press, 1984.

Eliot, T. S. *Selected Essays.* New York: Harcourt, Brace and Company, 1932.

Franz, Thomas R. Review of *Museo de cera. Hispania* 59 (March 1976): 174–75.

Friedrich, Hugo. *The Structure of Modern Poetry: From the Mid-Nineteenth Century to the Mid-Twentieth Century.* Translated by Joachim Neugroschel. Evanston, Ill.: Northwestern University Press, 1974.

Fuertes, Gloria. *Obras incompletas.* Madrid: Cátedra, 1983.

Gamoneda, Antonio. *Edad (Poesía 1947–1986).* Edited by Miguel Casado. Madrid: Cátedra, 1988.

García Martín, José Luis, ed. *La generación de los ochenta.* Valencia: Poesía Valencia, 1988.

Genette, Gérard. *Mimologiques: Voyage en Cratylie.* Paris: Seuil, 1976.

————. "Valéry and the Poetics of Language." *Textual Strategies*. Edited by Josué Harari. Ithaca: Cornell University Press, 1979, 359–73.

Gil de Biedma, Jaime. *El pie de la letra: Ensayos 1955–1979*. Barcelona: Editorial Crítica, 1980.

————. *Las personas del verbo*. Barcelona: Seix Barral, 1982.

Gimferrer, Pere. *Poemas: 1962–1969*. Madrid: Visor, 1988.

————. "La poesía última de Vicente Aleixandre." In Cano, ed. *Vicente Aleixandre*, 265–73.

Góngora, Luis de. *Sonetos completos*. Edited by Biruté Ciplijauskaité. Madrid: Castalia, 1969.

González, Angel. *Palabra sobre palabra*. Barcelona: Seix Barral, 1986.

Guillén, Jorge. *Cántico*. First complete edition. Buenos Aires: Sudamericana, 1950.

————. *El argumento de la obra*. Barcelona: Llibres de la Sinera, 1969.

————. *Lenguaje y poesía: Algunos casos españoles*. Madrid: Revista de Occidente, 1962.

Hart, Anita. "The Poet in José Angel Valente's Metapoetic Texts." *Hispanic Journal* 11, 2 (Fall 1990): 119–35.

Hassan, Ihab. *The Postmodern Turn: Essays in Postmodern Theory and Culture*. Columbus: Ohio State University Press, 1987.

Havard, Robert. *Jorge Guillén: Cántico*. London: Grant and Cutler, 1986.

Hoesterev, Ingeborg, ed. *Zeitgeist in Babel: The Postmodernist Controversy*. Bloomington: Indiana University Press, 1991.

Hosek, Chaviva and Patricia Parker, eds. *Lyric Poetry: Beyond New Criticism*. Ithaca: Cornell University Press, 1985.

Hutcheon, Linda. *The Poetics of Postmodernism: History, Theory, Fiction*. New York: Routledge, 1988.

Ilie, Paul. "Descent and Castration." In Daydí-Tolson, ed., *Vicente Aleixandre*, 104–21.

Jakobson, Roman. "Closing Statement: Linguistics and Poetics." *Semiotics: An Introductory Anthology*. Edited by Robert E. Innis. Bloomington: Indiana University Press, 1985, 147–75.

Jameson, Fredric. "Postmodernism and Consumer Society." In *The Anti-Aesthetic*. Edited by Hal Foster. Port Townsend, Wash.: Bay Press, 1983.

Jauristi, Jon. *Diario de un poeta recién cansado*. Pamplona: Pamiela, 1986.

Jiménez, José Olivio. *Diez años de poesía española: 1960–1970*. Madrid: Insula, 1972.

Lamillar, Juan. *Música oscura*. Sevilla: Renacimiento, 1984.

Langbaum, Robert. *Poetry of Experience*. New York: Random House, 1957.

Lanz, Juan José. "Por los caminos de la irracionalidad: notas sobre irrealismo e irracionalismo en la poesía de Jaime Gil de Biedma." *Insula* 523–24 (July–August 1990): 48–52.

López, Ignacio Javier. "Metonimia y negación: *Variaciones y figuras sobre un tema de La Bruyère* de Guillermo Carnero." *Hispanic Review* 54 (Summer 1986): 257–77.

————. "El silencio y la piedra: metáforas de la tradición en la poesía española contemporánea." *Bulletin of Hispanic Studies* 57 (January 1990): 43–56.

Mallarmé, Stéphane. *Oeuvres complètes*. Paris: Gallimard, 1945.

Marson, Ellen Engelson. *Poesía y poética de José Angel Valente*. New York: Eliseo Torres & Sons, 1978.

Martínez García, Francisco. *Historia de la literatura leonesa*. Madrid: Editorial Everest, 1982.

Mas, Miguel. *La escritura material de José Angel Valente*. Madrid: Hiperión, 1987.

Mayhew, Jonathan. *Claudio Rodríguez and the Language of Poetic Vision*. Lewisburg, Pa.: Bucknell University Press, 1990.

————. "El signo de la feminidad': Gender and Poetic Creation in José Angel Valente." *Revista de Estudios Hispánicos* 24, 2 (May 1991): 123–33.

Mazzaro, Jerome. *Postmodern American Poetry*. Urbana: Illinois University Press, 1980.

Miller, Martha Lafollette. "Claudio Rodríguez's Linguistic Skepticism: A Counterpart to Jorge Guillén Linguistic Faith." *Anales de la Literatura Española Contemporánea* 6 (1981): 105–21.

————. "Self-Commentary in Jorge Guillén's *Aire nuestro*." *Hispania* 65 (March 1982): 20–27.

Najt, Myriam. "La palabra 'palabra' en "La palabra del poeta." *Cuadernos Hispanoamericanos* 352–54 (October–December 1979). 581–93.

Novo Villaverde, Yolanda. In Daydí-Tolson, ed. *Vicente Aleixandre*, 122–44.

O'Hara, Frank. *The Collected Poems of Frank O'Hara*. Edited by Donald Allen. New York: Knopf, 1971.

Olson, Charles. *Additional Prose*. Edited by George F. Butterick. Bolinas, Calif.: Four Seasons Foundation, 1974.

Ong, Walter J. *Orality and Literacy: The Technologizing of the Word*. London and New York: Methuen, 1982.

Palley, Julian. *La luz no usada: La poesía de Pedro Salinas*. México: Andrea, 1966.

Paz, Octavio. *Children of the Mire: Modern Poetry from Romanticism to the Avant-Garde*. Cambridge: Harvard University Press, 1974.

————. *Corriente alterna*. México: Siglo Veintiuno, 1967.

————. *The Siren & the Seashell*. Translated by Lysander Kemp and Margaret Sayers Peden. Austin: University of Texas Press, 1976.

Perloff, Marjorie. *The Poetics of Indeterminacy: Rimbaud to Cage*. Princeton: Princeton University Press, 1981.

————. *The Dance of the Intellect: Studies in the Poetry of the Pound Tradition*. New York: Cambridge University Press, 1985.

Persin, Margaret. "The Metapoetic Text of Jorge Guillén." *Perspectives on Contemporary Literature* 8 (1982): 91–98.

————. *Recent Spanish Poetry and the Role of the Reader*. Lewisburg, Pa.: Bucknell University Press, 1987.

Polo de Bernabé, José Manuel. *Conciencia y lenguaje en la obra de Jorge Guillén*. Madrid: Alfar: 1977.

Pope, Randolph D. "Vicente Aleixandre y las limitaciones del lenguaje." In Daydí-Tolson, ed. *Vicente Aleixandre*, 245–57.

Provencio, Pedro. *Poéticas españolas contemporáneas: La generación del 50*. Madrid: Hiperión, 1988.

Puccini, Dario. *La palabra poética de Vicente Aleixandre.* Barcelona: Ariel, 1979.

Riera, Carme. *La escuela de Barcelona: Barral, Gil de Biedma, Goytisolo: el núcleo poético de la generación de los 50.* Barcelona: Anagrama, 1988.

Riffaterre, Michael. *Semiotics of Poetry.* Bloomington: Indiana University Press, 1984.

———. *Text Production.* New York: Columbia University Press, 1983.

Rodríguez, Claudio. *Desde mis poemas.* Madrid: Cátedra, 1984.

Rogers, Douglass. "Posturas del poeta ante su palabra en la España de posguerra." In *After the War: Essays on Recent Spanish Poetry.* Edited by Salvador Jiménez-Fajardo and John Wilcox. Boulder, Co.: Society of Spanish and Spanish-American Studies, 1988.

Rorty, Richard. *Contingency, Irony, and Solidarity.* New York: Cambridge University Press, 1989.

Rovira, Pere. *La poesía de Jaime Gil de Biedma.* Barcelona: Edicions de Mall, 1986.

Salinas, Pedro. *Poesías completas.* Barcelona: Barral, 1971.

Seoane, Xavier. "Sobre *Museo de cera.*" *Cuadernos Hispanoamericanos* 459 (September 1988): 69–78.

Sherno, Sylvia R. "The Paradox of Poetry in Blas de Otero's *Esto no es un libro.*" *Hispania* 70 (December 1987): 768–75.

Silver, Philip W. *La casa de Anteo: Estudios de poética hispánica (de Antonio Machado a Claudio Rodríguez)* Madrid: Taurus: 1985.

Soufas, C. Christopher Jr. *Conflict of Light and Wind: The Spanish Generation of 1927 and the Ideology of Poetic Form.* Middletown, Conn.: Wesleyan University Press, 1989.

Summerhill, Stephen J. "Spanish Poetry of the Eighties: Some Problems of Definition." *España Contemporánea* 2, 4 (Spring 1989): 101–12.

Stixrude, David. *The Early Poetry of Pedro Salinas.* Madrid: Castalia, 1975.

Ugalde, P. L. "Jose María Alvarez, o el arte de la cita." *Hora de poesía* 3 (May–June 1979): 33–36.

Valente, José Angel. *Al dios del lugar.* Barcelona: Tusquets, 1989.

———. *Entrada en materia.* Edited by Jacques Ancet. Madrid: Cátedra, 1985.

———. *El fulgor.* Madrid: Cátedra, 1984.

———. *Mandorla.* Madrid: Cátedra, 1982.

———. *Material memoria.* Barcelona: La Gaya Ciencia, 1979.

———. *Las palabras de la tribu.* Madrid: Siglo XXI, 1971.

———. *La piedra y el centro.* Madrid: Taurus, 1982.

———. *Punto cero: Poesía 1953–1979.* Barcelona: Barral, 1980.

———. *Tres lecciones de tinieblas.* Barcelona: La Gaya Ciencia, 1980.

Valéry, Paul. *Oeuvres.* 2 vols. Paris: Gallimard, 1960.

Villena, Luis Antonio de. "La luna, astro final del 'Primer Aleixandre'" (Algo sobre *Mundo a solas*)." *Insula* 368–69 (July–August 1977): 8, 33.

———, ed. *Postnovísimos.* Madrid: Visor, 1986.

Winters, Yvor. *In Defense of Reason.* New York: The Swallow Press and William Morrow and Company, 1947.

Young, Howard. "Jorge Guillén and the Language of Poetry." *Hispania* 46 (March 1963): 66–77.

Index